Joseph Hergesheimer

Twayne's United States Authors Series

Kenneth Eble, Editor

University of Utah

TUSAS 473

JOSEPH HERGESHEIMER
(1880–1954)
Photograph courtesy of the
Humanities Research Center,
University of Texas at Austin

Joseph Hergesheimer

By Victor E. Gimmestad

Illinois State University

Twayne Publishers • *Boston*

Joseph Hergesheimer

Victor E. Gimmestad

Copyright © 1984 by G. K. Hall & Company
All Rights Reserved
Published by Twayne Publishers
A Division of G. K. Hall & Company
70 Lincoln Street
Boston, Massachusetts 02111

Book Production by Marne B. Sultz

Book Design by Barbara Anderson

Printed on permanent/durable acid-free
paper and bound in the United States of
America

**Library of Congress Cataloging in
Publication Data**

Gimmestad, Victor E.
    Joseph Hergesheimer.

    (Twayne's United States authors series; TUSAS 473)
    Bibliography: p. 112
    Includes index.
    1. Hergesheimer, Joseph, 1880–1954—
Criticism and interpretation.
I. Title. II. Series.
PS3515.E628Z68   1984   813'.52   84-6581
    ISBN 0-8057-7414-9 (Twayne Publishers)

To Our Children
Carole, Vickie, Gary

Contents

About the Author

Victor E. Gimmestad did his undergraduate work at St. Olaf College, Northfield, Minnesota, and took his doctorate at the University of Wisconsin, majoring in American literature. He is a professor of English, retired from Illinois State University, Normal, Illinois, where he lectured in American literature and modern world literature. From 1960 to 1967 he was head of the Department of English. While on a year's leave of absence during 1968–1969, he served as chairman of the Department of English at California Lutheran College, Thousand Oaks, California. He has taught at St. Olaf College and in high schools in Minnesota, Wisconsin, and the Canal Zone. He is the author of *John Trumbull* (Twayne's United States Authors Series) and of articles on American literature in professional journals.

Preface

Although in 1922 Hergesheimer was voted America's foremost novelist, his reputation has declined so much that now he is scarcely known. In his day, he was one of this country's few aesthetes, and he was respected for his novels as well as for his articles, sketches, and numerous short stories. It is the aim of this monograph to explore his contribution to American literature and define his standing in it a half century after his last successful novel.

The present study is the first to include the entire corpus of Hergesheimer's work. It necessarily stresses the novels, including those published only in periodicals; but it covers also the shorter work which made him so popular with the American public. It traces the author's development by an examination of his published writings and of his manuscripts, particularly the excellent collection of correspondence at the Humanities Research Center at the University of Texas, a source apparently not available to Ronald E. Martin in his scholarly study.

Permission to quote from manuscripts has been granted by the Princeton University Library; Mrs. Margaret Freeman Cabell, Richmond, Virginia; the Clifton Waller Barrett Library, University of Virginia Library; the Beinecke Rare Book and Manuscript Library (Collection of American Literature), Yale University Library; and Dallett Hemphill, Attorney at Law, West Chester, Pennsylvania.

Other libraries that made their facilities and materials available and extended generous aid are: the Humanities Research Center, University of Texas (special thanks to David Farmer, Ellen Dunlap, and Sally Leach); the University of Illinois Library; Milner Library, Illinois State University; the Library of Congress; the University of Wisconsin Memorial Library; the Louis Round Wilson Library, University of North Carolina; the Enoch Pratt Free Library, Baltimore, Maryland; and the Houghton Library, Harvard University.

My greatest obligation has been to my wife, inspiration and co-worker.

Victor E. Gimmestad

Illinois State University

Chronology

Bright Shawl. Western tour resulting in "The Magnetic West." To Cuba to see the filming of *The Bright Shawl.*

1923   *The Presbyterian Child. Tol'able David* (published first in *SEP* in 1917). Restoration of the Dower House completed.

1924   *Balisand.* Change of style. Career began to decline.

1925   *From an Old House* (published first in *SEP* in 1925). Returned from Mexico where he had gone to make a a picture for Pola Negri at the government's request.

1926   *Tampico: A Novel* (published first in *Harper's Bazaar* in 1926). To Hollywood with H. L. Mencken.

1928   *Quiet Cities* (published first in *SEP* in 1927). *Tampico* produced as a stage play.

1929   *Swords and Roses* (published first in *SEP* in 1928). *Triall by Armes* (published first in *Scribner's Magazine* in 1927).

1930   *The Party Dress* (published first in *Cosmopolitan* in 1929). Serious illness.

1931   *The Limestone Tree* (published first in *SEP* in 1929). *Sheridan: A Military Narrative. Biography and Bibliographies* (published first in *Colophon* in 1931). Trip to Europe.

1932   *Berlin. Love in the United States* and *The Big Shot* (published first in *SEP* in 1929). Trip to Cuba.

1933   *Tropical Winter* (published first in *SEP* in 1931–1932).

1934   *The Foolscap Rose* (published first in *SEP* in 1933). To Mexico. To Europe.

1936   "Demeter, A Farm Woman" in *SEP* (last published novel). To London.

1942   Princeton exhibit.

1944   Lecture on "Christian Art" at the National Gallery of Art. Readership fell off. Only *The Three Black Pennys* and *Java Head* continued to sell.

1945   Sold the Dower House.

1950   "The Token" telecast.

1951   "Happy Birthday, Dear Mr. Cabell," in *Town & Country* (last published article).

1952   [Letter to the Editor] in *New York Times Book Review*

1954   Died April 25 at Sea Isle, New Jersey.

Chapter One

An American Aesthete

Joseph Hergesheimer was a prominent American novelist and short story writer in the late 1910s and the 1920s. Although relatively unknown today, he was so popular in 1922 that a *Literary Digest* poll of critics that year rated him the best contemporary author, considerably ahead of writers such as Eugene O'Neill.[1] As can be seen from the Hergesheimer Collection at the University of Texas, he was a prolific author. The collection contains 258 published entries, 25,000 pages of manuscripts and typescripts, and thirty-one titles of cataloged books and pamphlets for the period 1914–1934. It also includes 2,600 pieces of correspondence and numerous unpublished works, fiction and nonfiction, prose and poetry, plays and movie scenarios.[2] Along with James Branch Cabell, Carl Van Vechten, and Elinor Wylie, he was one of the few American aesthetes in his time.

His Life

On 15 February 1880 Joseph Hergesheimer was born into a solid, middle-class family in Germantown, Pennsylvania. When his father, an employee of the United States Coast and Geodetic Survey, was absent on duty, the mother took her son with her to live at Woodnest, the substantial home of her father, Thomas MacKellar, and his two sisters. MacKellar, a pious Scotch Presbyterian immigrant who had made his money in the type foundry business, was the dominant figure in the household.

Often ill, Hergesheimer missed all formal schooling except for about three years when he was enrolled at the Germantown Friends School, an orthodox Quaker institution, where he was undistinguished in both sports and academics. At seventeen he entered the Pennsylvania Academy of Fine Arts to study painting. There he worked in a desultory, unsuccessful way but nevertheless developed an interest in Impressionism.

When he was twenty-one, many of his elders died, and he received an inheritance from his deceased grandfather. He went to Italy ostensibly to study painting, but he led a sybaritic life in Venice, even having his initials embroidered in silver on the sleeves of his gondolier. After a year his inheritance was gone, and he returned to the United States with only twenty-five cents.

Following a brief return to the Academy and a moderate excursion into riotous living, he decided to change his life. He embarked on a walking tour, met Lucas Cleeve (pseudonym for Mrs. Adelina Kingscote), an English authoress, read galley proof for her, and decided that he could write better. The meeting with the once-popular but now forgotten Lucas Cleeve was pivotal, for Hergesheimer immediately began his years of uninterrupted composition.

Early in the century he corresponded with Miss Dorothy Hemphill, a relative of a fellow student at the Academy. On 14 November 1907, he and Dorothy were married in West Chester. Honeymooning in Italy, they underwent a temporarily difficult time when he had a nervous breakdown because his writing was not proceeding well. Following his recovery and further travel in Europe, the couple returned to the United States.

After his marriage, as before, he wrote compulsively; he said he wrote the day before his marriage and the day after. During the entire period from 1899 to 1913 he struggled to write salable material; and, hampered by inadequate education and lack of guidance, he stumbled toward improvement. In 1913 he finally sold three pieces to the *Forum*,[3] and two years later he established his long and profitable connection with the *Saturday Evening Post.* Living by the stormy Atlantic in the winter of 1913–1914, he wrote *The Lay Anthony*, and in the spring he and Dorothy moved into the Dower House in West Chester. Later in 1914 the novel was published, and it was followed by *Mountain Blood* the next year. The books were not financial successes, but they did call the attention of critics such as H. L. Mencken and Llewellyn Jones to a new talent.

The zenith of his writing career began with the appearance of *The Three Black Pennys* in 1917. Within seven years he published *Java Head, Linda Condon, San Cristóbal de la Habana, Cytherea, The Bright Shawl, The Presbyterian Child*, and *Balisand*; he turned out numerous stories and articles for magazines, especially the *Saturday Evening Post*; he worked occasionally for the movie industry; he attempted writing plays; he gave lectures; and he wrote introductions to books.

These years were extremely busy for Hergesheimer. He traveled about the United States and to Cuba more than once. In 1922 he was sent to Midwestern and Western states by George Horace Lorimer, publisher of the *Saturday Evening Post*, a trip which resulted in the nine-part series "The Magnetic West." Along with Van Vechten, Cabell, and Mencken, he supported Emily Clark's Richmond literary magazine, *The Reviewer*, by writing frequent articles and soliciting others from authors such as John Galsworthy. To this period also belongs the rebuilding of the Dower House. And during this time, when he was characterized as a "charming egotist" by Scott Fitzgerald,[4] he was known for his sartorial elegance, especially his neckties and his finely tailored suits. His appearance, his writings, and his manners were captured impressionistically by Florine Stettheimer in a portrait depicting him as a voluptuous aesthete.

Once Hergesheimer had gained some attention as a writer, he met other members of the literary world. At first he may have been given to monologue instead of dialogue when talking with them, for, according to Burton Rascoe, "He talked about himself, his work, his plans with gusto, and with a touch of amusing vanity and conceit, never irritatingly, but like an unsophisticated, very ambitious, very self-conscious youngster. He was naive in his self-centeredness, and so bland about it, so far from being dogmatic, ill-mannered or over-assertive, that one took him into one's heart."[5] With his scanty formal education, Hergesheimer was intrigued by ideas new to him, such as platonic love, and discoursed on them at length. But in a few years he became an adept conversationalist by conscious effort, expertly drawing out his interlocutors' ideas. He had then achieved his own stated goal for conversations of "gilding the charms of women and magnifying the eminence of men...."[6]

With close friends such as Van Vechten he discussed technical problems of writing, and frequently talked about the work of the English aesthete George Moore. In a group he often dazzled his listeners with his verbal pyrotechnics and scintillating observations. As characterized by Van Vechten, "He was brilliantly articulate and his conversation was as arresting as the iridescent plumage of a bird of paradise, indeed one might say as his own prose. 'There are only a few of us left,' he would allege incisively, and that would lead him into glorious imaginative flights which found us, his companions, a little breathless."[7] Unfortunately, Van Vechten did not record more sayings. Rascoe described the nature of some gems as "minute, suggestive, colorful descriptions of people and places,"[8] and Sara Haardt noted his ability to characterize accurately a setting such as a crowded restaurant.[9] An example of Hergesheimer's gift for pungent observation is found in an exchange of letters with Julian Boyd, librarian at Princeton, in which it is confirmed that the author had indeed said Toynbee had buried civilization in an Episcopalian graveyard.[10] Not only Van Vechten but others such as Emily Clark, Rascoe, and Huntington Cairns paid tribute to the brilliant oral statements, which continued to flow long after Hergesheimer lost the ability to write stories.

At the height of his popularity, Hergesheimer's speeches lost him many friends because of his desire to shock or surprise. Though Mencken trod on the sensibilities of the "booboisie" steadily, he had his admirers; Hergesheimer, however, had less success. In Boston he offended a convention of booksellers by telling the assemblage, "Bookselling is the only profession . . . in which such colossal ignorance is displayed by those engaged in it."[11] In 1921 he delivered a talk to the Charlotte Cushman Club about a fictitious author; and in the same year he delivered "The Feminine Nuisance in American Literature" as the Bergen lecture at Yale.[12] He admired beautiful women of vitality in fiction, but he had little praise for women as readers, and he condemned them for cheapening American fiction. He injudiciously asserted that "literature in the United States is being strangled with a petticoat."[13] Such appearances, as well as comments that "a marcel is the chief difference between women and other animals,"[14] began to alienate his readership and hurt his book sales. Fortunately for him, Alfred A. Knopf, his publisher, persuaded him to stop giving talks.

At the peak of his career Hergesheimer had a large circle of friends, and there was much social activity at the Dower House. Because several of his stories were adapted by the movie industry, he became acquainted with the Hollywood stars Lillian Gish, Aileen Pringle, Mary Pickford, Douglas Fairbanks, Anita Loos, Norma Shearer, and Richard Barthelmess, several of whom visited the Hergesheimers at West Chester. Among his closest literary friends, all in the East, he numbered Sinclair Lewis in the early years; Cabell, literary confidante; Van Vechten; and Mencken, a convivial confrere from 1914 to 1954—being, in fact, as Mencken's secretary wrote Hergesheimer's widow, the "closest friend" Mencken had.[15]

After 1924 his career began to decline. While he had been one of the first to recognize that there was a new audience after World War I, he did not capture the new mood of disillusionment as well as did Sinclair Lewis, Scott Fitzgerald, Ernest Hemingway, John Dos Passos, and William Faulkner. His principal books during this period were *From an Old House, Tampico, Quiet Cities, Swords and Roses, The Party Dress, The Limestone Tree, Sheridan: A Military Narrative, Berlin*, and *The Foolscap Rose*. Because of his lessening creative strength and the radical change in taste with the coming of the Great Depression, he had difficulty getting his stories accepted from 1930 on; and he published no more novels after 1936. His last published article was a tribute to his friend Cabell in 1951. From 1947 to 1951 he had a Bollingen Foundation award to write an autobiography, but it has not been printed.

As the 1920s waned and Hergesheimer's interests changed, he no longer wanted new friends or acquaintances; he yearned even more strongly for the peace of the uncomplicated past. He lost interest in fiction as he began to read widely in history, philosophy, and religion. Then in 1945 the Dower House was sold for financial reasons, and the Hergesheimers moved to a cottage on the Atlantic shore at Stone Harbor, New Jersey. On 25 April 1954 he died in a nearby hospital.

Influences

First among the major influences on the young Hergesheimer was the household at Woodnest, his grandfather's home. After spending much of childhood and youth in it, he later recalled he had had "a rotten time" and that his parents were no more prepared for their responsibility than they were for keeping "an elephant or a Stiegel flip glass."[16] At Woodnest he lived in an atmosphere of the past, surrounded by persons most of whom were two generations older—his grandfather and his great-aunts. In *A Presbyterian Child* he recalled the strict, religious grandfather leading prayers or at the organ playing hymns, the afternoon rides in a horse-drawn carriage, the tower on the house, the rock garden, flowers, and pink dogwood. And important also as a model of rigidly controlled conduct was his great-aunt Henrietta, who turned her face to the wall as she died so that she would still be in command of her appearance. The powerful religious training resulted in an emphasis on the transience of earthly life, the wages of sin, and the importance of sound principles. Though he lost the theology he learned in childhood, he retained the feeling and ethic of the family religion.

His father's absence and his mother's withdrawal after the deaths of three of her children left Hergesheimer much to his own resources; and being without playmates or schooling most of the time, he occasionally turned to fantasy, such as the following vision of a romance: "I couldn't remember what I had hoped for, probably an entrancing adventure of the heart, the miraculous advent of a loveliness in white and with her hair up. I am afraid I thought of her as luxurious in circumstance, with a carriage and pair, both of horses and men on the box, conveniently waiting for us. And then we'd roll away from reality to a great marble house far back on an emerald lawn . . . up the winding tan bark drive, past screens of copper beeches, to the porte-cochere."[17]

His reading played a dominant role in his writing career. Although his grandfather's library contained dozens of literary volumes, such as Thackeray, Dickens, and Trollope,[18] he disliked such books and read fiction which he later considered "trash"—novels by the Duchess, Ouida (Marie Louise de la Rámee, 1840–1908), G. A. Henty (forty to fifty), Kirk Monroe, Edward Ellis, and Howard Pyle, whose *Man of Iron*, his favorite, he enjoyed rereading even in his thirties. Though he read inferior fiction, according to one scholar he liked good poetry: "From the years of thirteen or fourteen he later recalled Keats's 'Eve of St. Agnes,' 'Ode to [sic] a Grecian Urn,' and 'La Belle Dame sans Merci'; and Coleridge's 'The Ancient Mariner' and 'Christabel.' He remembered Dante G. Rossetti's 'The Blessed Damozel' and Matthew Arnold's 'Dover Beach' and 'The Scholar Gypsy'; Ernest Dowson's 'Cynara' and Arthur Symons' *London Nights*. Also, Verlaine's poems in translation made a 'deep impression at some early time.' "[19] Between fourteen and seventeen he often perused *The Yellow Book* and *The Savoy*, the English aesthetes' magazines. In early adulthood he turned progressively to Joseph Conrad, Turgenev, Jeremy Taylor, George Moore, and then "practically nothing."[20] By his late thirties he thought Conrad, George Moore, and Turgenev were the most important to him. In his writings he was little affected by the Great

Books, study of which he once called an "intermittent wake on dead works."[21]

Hergesheimer indicates his own preferences at times in his comments on other authors, some of whom were influences on him. He praised Conrad for picturesque spectacle in *Youth* and *Nostromo*; George Moore for dissociating the beautiful from the moral;[22] Stephen Crane for impressionistic descriptions and for minimizing Henry Fleming as an individual in *The Red Badge of Courage*;[23] and Turgenev for his portrayal of women. It is noteworthy that he did not mention Henry James, who frequently was thought to have affected his writing. But any influence by James was exerted through Conrad, if at all, because Hergesheimer had a philosophy of writing different from that of James: he urged that not ideas or moral purpose but rather the "fundamental emotions" should be the criterion by which literature is evaluated.[24] Furthermore, in the early twenties he said that he had read fifteen pages of James five years earlier and five pages fifteen years in the past.[25]

His interest in painting also greatly affected his writing. Despite his own lack of success in the field, he was swayed so strongly by his training at the Academy of Fine Arts that his entire approach to writing was colored by it. In his words, he had never been "able to quite get away from either art or Presbyterianism. . . . The Presbyterianism burns in, sporadically."[26] Hugh Walpole, Mrs. Amélie Troubetzkoy, and Mencken pointed to the pictorial conception of his novels and even of the travelog *Berlin*, published in 1932. Their observations were in agreement with Hergesheimer's intentions because he began with a picture and went from that to character. He gathered details not only because they gave accuracy but, he said, because "they are like colors on my palette; more than that, they help me not only to express my people but to conceive their mental processes."[27] The particular pictorial quality he sought was akin to that of the Impressionists. As he told James Joseph Napier years later, he strove in writing for the effects obtained in painting by an artist closely allied to them—Degas.[28]

For Hergesheimer these effects were to be stirred emotions which were carefully arranged in writings such as "The Magnetic West." What he was interested in was not so much realism as the author's reaction to "life," and in the reader he sought to obtain the same reactions from words that he would have had from an actual experience.[29] He seems to have been so completely devoted to his goal that he gave up his attempts to write movie scenarios because, as he wrote to Lillian Gish (7 January 1921), for him they were mere statements of acts rather than the creation of emotions.

One of the deepest influences on the author was the venerable Dower House, which dated from 1712. Only *The Lay Anthony* and *Mountain Blood* among his novels were written without its coloring mood. The nature of Hergesheimer responded favorably to the house, and he wrote his best books while living in it; indeed, he said the house had written the volumes. *The Three Black Pennys* and *Java Head* were the first novels composed under its influence, and they are his best. *From an Old House*, written after the eighteen-month rebuilding process, tells not only of the antique desks, sofa, beds, and Stiegel glass but also of the restoration with an emphasis on fine details such as handmade screws, wooden pegs, old hinges, cypress shingles, and slate over the chimneys which reminded him of quiet, courageous, and honest days. The house brought out in him the antiquarian taste evident as early as 1913.[30] As his interests changed, he wanted more and more to write about Americana. He felt a nostalgic yearning for both the vanished beauty of the past and the rugged virtues. For him, the stone-walled Dower House, embodying the best of preceding American centuries, was a resource, a sustainer, an inspiration. *From an Old House* is a loving tribute written from the very core of his being.

Writing Practices

Feeling driven to compose, Hergesheimer seems to have written continually from the time he was nineteen, whether he was at the beach, on a yacht, in the Virginia mountains, in Philadelphia, or in West Chester. We know little of his early habits of composition except that he destroyed all he wrote but a few pages. In the Virginia mountains at Monterey (Greenstream) he revised and retyped his manuscript so often that he had it memorized and recited long passages to the trout in the streams he fished. Later, after his years of apprenticeship, he wrote with more ease and needed to revise only slightly while turning out 2,500 words per day at first, and then 3,000. He revised the typescript many times, of course, and sometimes made an inordinate number of alterations in the galley proofs.

In the early days at West Chester he worked at the Dower House in a room overlooking the golf course; later he composed in an office downtown or, at one time, in a small house he owned. At the Dower House and at Stone Harbor in his last years he kept searching for an elusive exact word despite the pain of making repeated revisions with an arthritic forefinger.

Like Sir Walter Scott, Hergesheimer provided a realistic background for his tales of the past. To attain this, he did research by reading and by direct experience. He read an enormous amount and took thousands of notes himself or employed research workers to do so. He read, for instance, about early iron production in America, about Salem and its shipping in the 1840s, about eighteenth-century Virginia, and about Kentucky history. But he was not content with reading alone: he worked in the steel mills for six weeks before writing *Tubal Cain, The Three Black Pennys,* and "Steel"; he visited Salem and had his typescript checked for facts before printing *Java Head*; and he traveled to New England for "The Dark Fleece," to Virginia for *Balisand,* and to Kentucky for *The Limestone Tree.* He insisted on accurate detail so much that some critics mistook him for a historical novelist and misjudged him accordingly; but, as he wrathfully insisted to Sinclair Lewis, he was not attempting to be one.[31] Having a different goal, he consulted the standard American histories, books by specialists, and contemporary records and visited actual settings not only to provide accuracy but also, if possible, to capture the spirit of the earlier times.

Audience

Hergesheimer wrote for two different audiences: artistic, sensitive persons and the readers of popular magazines. For himself and a select few, those with the "sense of beauty and fitness" he and Cabell possessed,[32] he tried to capture moods and emotions so that he would achieve a third dimension. He strove for effects other than the merely factual; though he was known as an expert portrayer of decorative surfaces, he sought to be more than that. Eventually he thought that for this audience the novel as a form was inadequate to portray multidimensional life. In 1928 he wrote that he was seeking a written vehicle other than the novel,[33] which he told Ferris Greenslet, Houghton Mifflin editor, he had come to regard as "stupid" (27 December 1928).

For the second audience he composed short stories which appeared in the popular magazines. He did so largely because he had very expensive tastes, which could be satisfied only by a large income impossible to earn by book royalties alone. As he later wrote Knopf (21 November 1939), during his best times he made $100,000 a year, mainly from periodical writing. When some of his friends questioned his writing for periodicals, he defended himself, insisting to Mencken that he had not suffered from it (13 August 1917), to John Galsworthy that periodical writing was not "inferior" but "circumscribed" (29 November 1921), and to Cabell that he had always avoided vulgarization which to him meant a cheap appeal to passion (18 October 1921). But he recognized that the different audience affected his work when he said that a rewriting of "Steel" would entail changes "in a way impossible to the pages of a general magazine."[34] Furthermore, Hergesheimer's view that stories in periodicals necessarily were "circumscribed" seems contradicted by the appearance of *Java Head* and *Linda Condon* in popular magazines before book publication. He felt the sting of criticism, however, and insisted to Cabell that in 1920 and 1921 he had turned out a few short stories and spent most of his time improving his books.

Aesthete

Under the influence of the Impressionistic painters, George Moore, *The Yellow Book*, and *The Savoy*, Hergesheimer wrote as an aesthete through the 1910s and 1920s, maintaining a devotion to a vague, attractive, multiformed ideal—beauty. Thoroughly devoted to this ideal, he found pursuing it in a United States cherishing moral goals a difficult task, as he complained to Galsworthy (29 November 1921). Among his writing friends he saw only Cabell and Van Vechten as having a similar aim; but he insisted that any imaginative man always has a vision of "an ultimate loveliness," an "instinctively Platonic gesture,"[35] such as that in *Linda Condon*. On a more mundane level he spoke of beauty as a quality "that pinches the heart and interferes with breathing."[36] Frequently he incorporated elaborate decors into his novels and they too were meant to appeal aesthetically.

From the very beginning, though, he included in his sense of beauty both courage in facing the human predicament and lost loveliness. Howat Penny I of *The Three Black Pennys*, Gerrit Ammidon of *Java Head*, Richard Bale of *Balisand*, and Govett Bradier of *Tampico* are persons who illustrate his conception that "beauty is the quality of a courageous purpose maintained against the hopeless and transitory aspects of life and death."[37] In practice he added to this definition a lost loveliness, as can be observed in his novels about the past and in his 1930 preface to *The Three Black Pennys.*

During most of his writing career his goal was aesthetic pleasure with no admixture of didacticism. As he interpreted "pleasure," it emphasized feeling rather than intellect and frequently limited the scope of his novels to two dimensions. But he lost interest in aestheticism after his severe illness in 1930, and he began extensive reading in history and philosophy.

Chapter Two

Apprentice Novels

Although Hergesheimer, as a compulsive writer, may have found novels such as those by Lucas Cleeve easy to compose, he found that selling them to a publisher was difficult. He wrote some that he could not market, such as the lost "Ellen Dayton," which John Long considered publishing in 1905,[1] and "Annot in the World" (1912), which exists in typescript. It was not until 1914, when he was thirty-four, that he saw a book of his in print—*The Lay Anthony*—published by Mitchell Kennerley. The next year he had the pleasure of seeing *Mountain Blood* on the market and thereby gained attention as an author of promise.

The Lay Anthony

The Lay Anthony, dedicated to his wife Dorothy as "This Figment of a Perpetual Flowering" and later called by the author "the outcome of neo-platonic poetry,"[2] seems to have arisen in idealistic youthful dreams of romance. A contemporary novel of continuous action, it narrates the love of young Anthony Ball for Eliza Dreen and his maintaining his purity, especially after her declaration, " 'It would be wonderful to care for just one person, *always*,' she continued intently: 'I had a dream when I was quite young. . . . I dreamed that a marvellous happiness would follow a constancy like that.' "[3] The novel does not portray such a happiness but rather the ethereal possibility described in the epigraph from Boccaccio: ". . . *if in passing from this deceitful world into true life love is not forgotten, . . . I know that among the most joyous souls of the third heaven my Fiametta sees my pain. Pray her, if the sweet draught of Lethe has not robbed me of her, . . . to obtain my ascent to her.*" It is this youthful, spiritual love to which the book appears to be a tribute.

Purity. In telling his story Hergesheimer uses white lilacs as a recurring symbol of purity and of Eliza, who not only dreams of constancy and affection but embodies them for the short time before she dies of pneumonia. Anthony Ball, the protagonist, is a shiftless amateur mechanic of good family who is unfortunate: the garage fails, his pitching before a major league scout is a disaster, and his dancing irritates his partner. Nevertheless, he is not a bad fellow at heart, as he shows in his handyman jobs for a Mrs. Bosbyshell. When in leaving a drugstore on an intended group visit to a brothel he breaks a case of white lilac perfume, he is kept pure by the confusion and expense of the accident. Then on a picnic Eliza Dreen brings an armful of white lilacs, and for Tony this creates a continuous association of these flowers with her.

When Tony's father sends him on a train to California, Tony goes partway, takes employment as a chauffeur with a philanderer, and is almost seduced by one of the ladies in the wayward party; but the scent of white lilacs saves him. Leaving the group, Tony is robbed by a madman but finds work with an aging scientist experimenting with Mendelian law. Annot Hardinge, the daughter, attempts to lead Tony astray but the fragrance of white lilacs, which strengthens his resolve, and her casual attitude toward love cause him to reject her. Immediately leaving that job, Tony learns that he inherited $47,000 from Mrs. Bosbyshell and that Eliza had died at the time Tony went west. Traumatically shocked, Tony gets drunk, smells lilacs and thinks he hears Eliza calling him to a heavenly love, and in a protest against God enters a brothel to lose his purity. There he attempts to save a girl from being forced into white slavery, is shot, and dies with his idealistic dream of Eliza intact.

Analysis and estimate. Though it does reveal many traits to be found in the succeeding novels, this first novel by Hergesheimer is *sui generis*; the author himself pointed to the book's distinctiveness in his canon when he once inscribed on a flyleaf, "Here the illusion of reality of later works of the imagination is corrected by the reality of illusion."[4] He apparently strove for an effect from the combining of scent with the adolescent dream of a heavenly union of Eliza and Tony. Here the protagonists die young, when they are in full flower, like the white lilacs.

As in all of Hergesheimer's novels, the characters are sharply drawn, so that there is no confusion among them. Although the author has a few literary allusions (Virgil, Thomas Gray, Richard Sheridan), the novel is not enriched by them; but it is dominated by the epigraph from Boccaccio. In these apprentice days Hergesheimer used more figurative language than he later did but it was not distinguished and is well represented by comparisons such as "he whistled like an old hinge" (79). Of all his novels, this first one along with *Linda Condon* was based on literature (Renaissance); several, including his best, were based on historical research. Because the range of the novel is narrow, the reader feels that the story is not fully developed, just as he reacts to many of the author's later novels. Here, though, the ethereal love theme militates against ample development and realism is needed to anchor the intangible. The reader is puzzled by the fifty-six chapters in a relatively short book and suspects that the author's strength lay less in a sense of form and more in individual words, which appear to be chosen at times for their sound, such as Hydrangea House and Mrs. Bosbyshell. In this novel, too, one sees something of Hergesheimer's attitude toward life—Tony receives word of the inherited $47,000 and Eliza's death at almost the same moment, creating a bitter irony.

For his initial novel, *The Lay Anthony* demonstrated incorporation of a worthwhile literary idea, effective use of a symbol, and skill in handling the distorted point of view. Tony's experiences in the tavern and on the street appear written from the inside. The scene involving the celebrating couples at the restaurant is melodramatic, and the one at Tony's death is also. More serious is the fact that Tony maintains his purity by luck and the memory-stirring scent of lilacs at the drugstore, at the restaurant, at Hardinges', and at the brothel. And the sudden love of the sophisticated Eliza for the uncultivated Tony seems implausible. The diction reveals traces of his earlier ornate *Forum* pieces: "The glass doors to the fire-engine house stood open, the machines glimmering behind a wide demilune of chairs holding a motley assemblage of men" (16) and "He breathed stentoriously amid his exertions, muttering objurgations in connection with the name of an absent servitor, hopelessly drunk, Anthony gathered, in the stable" (157). There were also what Professor William Lyon Phelps called "crudities"[5] in such mistakes as "practicable" for "practical" and some other weaknesses pointed out in the best reviews, those written by Mencken in *Smart Set*[6] and by Llewellyn Jones, literary editor of the *Chicago Evening Post*.[7]

Perhaps the two most questionable stylistic traits are the unnecessary use of the full name and that which Cabell termed appositional. In *The Lay Anthony* the only example of the first is the repetition

of Rufus Hardinge. But there are many examples of the second, such
as "a huge conspiracy against his success, his happiness" (28), "they
did not offer adequate material, aim, for the years" (29), and a loco-
motive headlight's flaring "unexpectedly, whitely" (136). Cabell
seems to account for some of these when he calls them appositional,
but it often appears that the second word is coordinate, and at times
it could well be qualifying. Whatever the intention, the practice may
stem from the author's fondness for words, a liking which may have
led him into unduly savoring them. Eventually these mannerisms
of Hergesheimer's mature style led one critic to write a caustically
satirical article, "Narcissa Baddery (How to hergesheimer [*sic*], *in one
easy lesson*)."[8] Hergesheimer's continued and later expanded use of
this trait makes the reader think it must have been a touch of which
he was proud. Often, though, the reader is reminded of another brush
stroke, possibly an attempt to improve the composition.

Mountain Blood

In his second novel Hergesheimer depicted the wages of sin in
the valleys and mountains which he had come to know through long
stays in Monterey, Virginia, or as he summarized it, it concerned
"The failure of an aged man to repair a spiritual wrong with gold."[9]
To portray lust and avarice as evil and fatal, he chose Gordon Makimmon, a shiftless, brawling, stagecoach driver from a family that had
little except pride in what he called their "mountain blood." In the
author's longer fiction Gordon has the distinction of being the only
common man used as a protagonist, for even Tony Ball came from
a well-to-do family.

In this volume of realistic regionalism, the only one Hergesheimer
wrote, Monterey and the surrounding area provided the setting and
characters. Added to these were several elements from Woodnest:
"The Arkansas Traveller," a song his father repeatedly played on
the violin; the description of the ice storm; and religious piety always
concerned with the struggle between good and evil. Both the realistic
regionalism and the religious note in the theme were uncharacteristic
of Hergesheimer.

Mountain Blood, dedicated to the author's mother, has many short
chapters which have been grouped in three parts, with time gaps
between, presaging a common successful practice in many of the later

novels from *The Three Black Pennys* to *The Limestone Tree*. The
omniscient author tells the story from the point of view of the main
character.

The wages of sin.   In the opening pages Hergesheimer brings
several important characters together and initiates subsequent action.
First we see Gordon driving the stage out of Stenton (Staunton) for
the fifty-mile trip to Greenstream (Monterey), the village where he
lives. Among the passengers are Lettice Hollidew, just graduated from
high school, and Buckley Simmons, son of a Greenstream merchant.
They are the offspring of the two wealthy men in the village, Pompey
Hollidew and Valentine Simmons, men who squeeze the valley's
inhabitants dry with usury. Gordon belongs to the group squeezed by
them. When Buckley insults Lettice on a steep grade, Gordon slashes
his face, seemingly by accident.

Returned to Greenstream, Gordon soon learns his gallantry in
defending Lettice and his perennial improvidence have ruined him.
Angered over his son's disfigurement, Valentine insists that Gordon
pay a substantial part of his debt and causes him to lose his job on
the stage. Unable to pay $250 in a few days, Gordon hikes to Spruce-
sap, West Virginia, to gamble; but most of his winnings go for the
dying sister Clare's hospitalization; and he loses his home in a sheriff's
sale. After Clare's funeral Gordon goes on a spree and throws away
over nine hundred dollars left from the house sale before coming
back to Greenstream destitute. At the Universalist minister's home he
meets the tempting Meta Beggs, the local schoolteacher. He courts
Lettice; and one Sunday, discovering that her father, Pompey, is lying
dead in his house, he rushes to her out in the country and persuades
her to marry him before she learns the news. The love of money by
Gordon has triumphed over principle.

Some months later the profligate Gordon orders a new suit, buys a
two-hundred-dollar dog, neglects the pregnant Lettice, and flirts with
Meta Beggs. A rendezvous with her at a camp meeting leads to a
dispute in which someone reduces Buckley to imbecility by hitting
his head with a thrown rock. Then later at a sap boiling Gordon and
Meta are confronted by the pregnant Lettice, who dies after the rough
buggy trip home. His toying with carnal desire has cost Lettice her life.

Over a year later Gordon sees a young girl weeping at a sheriff's
sale and finds she and her husband are being sold out for debt, just
as he had been. Because to him her voice and face seem like Lettice's,
he impulsively buys the young couple's farm and tells them to pay

him when they are able. Following this, he makes a career of helping the people impoverished by the usurers; but he loses his money to the scheming, unscrupulous Simmons; and, back as a stagecoach driver, he is fatally wounded when the imbecilic Buckley whips a horse and the rig tumbles into a canyon. After the confused and weak Gordon stumbles back to Greenstream, he dies with his hands on the bed where Lettice expired, having atoned only partly for succumbing to avarice and lust.

Analysis and estimate. In this episodic and contemporary novel the reader senses the author's concern for the technique of telling a story, the concern Van Vechten later said Hergesheimer perennially evinced when in literary company. Here, before his popularity, he made the modest change of using a three-part division, an experiment he continued successfully in *The Three Black Pennys* and in some later volumes. The tripartite structure provided both balance and chronological change.

An indication that Hergesheimer was still learning his trade lies in *Mountain Blood*'s style. When critics speak of it, they usually mean that which he used from 1917 to 1922; but he had several styles at his command, as he demonstrated clearly in his early writings. In the prose poems immediately preceding the novels he wrote ornate sentences he later considered filigree: "Against the star-girdled, velvet skirt of night, festooned with strings of swaying lanterns, the electric fountain cascades its golden bubbles into a black pool; the gold sinks to rose, to a misty, violet veil shimmering about luminous swords of white water."[10] Soon afterward, in *The Lay Anthony*, he wrote: "When she [Annot] left the car he slowly backed and circled to the carriage house. As he splashed body and wheels with water, polished the metal, dried and dusted the cushions, the crisp, cool voice of Annot Hardinge rang in his ears. He divined something of her isolated existence, her devotion to the absorbed, kindly man who was her father, and speculated upon her matured youth" (225). Here in a narrative he depended less on adjectival splendor.

The style of *Mountain Blood* is improved over that of its predecessor, but it is not consistent. In some descriptive passages, for example, the painter's terminology is prominent: "The sun sank toward the western range; the late afternoon grew hushed, as rich in color, in vert shadows, ultramarine, and amber, as heavy in foliage bathed in aureate light, as the nave of a cathedral under stained glass."[11] Or there is the similarity to writers such as Mary Noailles Murfree in

a passage providing an adjective for every noun: "A long table was
occupied by an industrious company that broke the absorbed silence
only by explosive requests for particularized dishes" (24). At times
faulty diction yields words such as "pellucid" and "gracile," not
suited to a backward mountain area. There is an unnecessary use of
the proper name with the pronoun: ". . . he, Gordon Makimmon,
held the deciding vote in the affairs of his home" (155). But more
important, the mannerisms which became so ingrained in his style
are here accentuated. In *The Lay Anthony* only one person was repeatedly called by his full name, but in *Mountain Blood* the last names
of Lettice, Pompey, Gordon, Valentine, and Meta often are used.
There also is more of the "appositional" style of which Cabell complained.

In *The Lay Anthony* Hergesheimer employed a distorted point of
view at the end when Tony has learned of Eliza's death. Here in
Mountain Blood he proves his skill in its use by portraying Gordon's
fight with three gamblers, a passage incorporating the nightmarish
quality found also in "Wild Oranges":

Jake swung the little, flexuous club softly against his palm, and Gordon
suddenly realized that the cripple intended to kill him.—That was the
lust which transfigured the gambler's countenance, which lit the fires
in the deathly cheeks, set the long fingers shaking. Gordon considered the
idea, and, obscurely, it troubled him, moved him a space from his apathy.
Instinctively, in response to a sudden movement of the figure above him,
he drew his arm up in front of his head; and an intolerable pain shot up
through his shoulder and flared, blindingly, in his eyes. It pierced his indifference, set in motion his reason, his memory; he realized the necessity,
the danger, of his predicament . . . the money!—he must guard it, take
it back with him. Above, in a heated, orange mist, the woman's face
loomed blank and inhuman; farther back Mr. Ottinger's features were
indistinctly visible. (66–67)

The regional elements and local color are among the better aspects
of the novel, although the story lacks the artistic detachment as well
as understanding and compassion of notable local-color artists such
as Sarah Orne Jewett. Hergesheimer flavors the book with a few
piquant localisms such as "caution to Dunkards" (226), "in a day
on a horse" (226), and "she'll fool you all over the mountain" (235).
Incorporating a camp meeting and sap boiling (both events providing
emotional release for the area's inhabitants), he made these events

pivotal, for Gordon met the tempting Meta Beggs at both, Buckley had his skull broken at the camp meeting, and Lettice confronted Meta and Gordon at the sap boiling. Thus the two gatherings are joined to the plot with a strong emotional link. It is in the characters, though, that the regional flavor attains its greatest strength, particularly in Gordon. A descendant of the Scotch who had poured into the mountain valleys many years earlier, Gordon, despite his pride, male chauvinism, insensitivity, and flirtatiousness, has determination and an instinct to protect the helpless, whether they be the schoolgirl Lettice, his sister Clare, or the natives exploited by the money-lenders. In his indecision over Lettice and Meta he was, in the author's language, "vaguely conscious of the baseness of the mere weighing of such a choice; but he was engulfed in his overmastering egotism; his sense of obligation was dulled by the supreme selfishness of a life-time [*sic*], of a life-time [*sic*] of unbridled temper and appetite, of a swaggering self-esteem which the remorseless operation of fate had ignored, and passed indifferently by, leaving him in complete ignorance of the terrible and grim possibilities of human mischance" (247). With his improvidence, foolishness, and occasional nobility, Gordon typifies a large segment of the valley folk.

In the minor characters the regionalism is equally pronounced. The author used them to provide a moral norm at times, almost like a Greek chorus, as, for example, the Caleys' disapproval of Gordon immediately after Lettice's death. Hergesheimer makes Sim Caley represent one type of rural native—independent, hard-drinking, and hard-working. In William Vibard, a distant relative of Gordon's, he illustrated the buffoonish folly of some valley residents. By holding back a small amount of grocery money from Gordon over a period of time, Vibard's wife saved enough so that her husband could buy ten accordions at once, a lifetime supply for his attempts to learn "The Arkansas Traveller." Hergesheimer does not glamorize or sentimentalize the valley people but reveals their boorishness, shift-lessness, wastefulness, and occasional cruelty. The tormenting of the newly arrived dog reveals a sadistic streak close to that of the loafers in *Huckleberry Finn* who awaken thoroughly only when some animal is being tormented.

Among the female characters, Lettice and Meta are clearly deline-ated and, in Hergesheimer's customary manner, strongly contrasted. According to Cabell, Lettice was so well done that she typified numer-ous innocent young girls in the area (15 November [1919]). Meta

Beggs, on the other hand, is the opposite of love and trust, and she
is not individualized but universalized. In one of his better rhetorical
passages Hergesheimer describes her as

the mask, smooth and sterile, of the hunger for adornment, for gold
bands and jewels and perfume, for goffered linen and draperies of silk
and scarlet. She was the naked idler stained with antimony in the clay
courts of Sumeria; the Paphian with painted feet loitering on the roofs
of Memphis while the blocks of red sandstone floated sluggishly down the
Nile for the pyramid of Khufu the King; she was the flushed voluptuousness relaxed in the scented spray of pagan baths; the woman with
piled and white-powdered hair in a gold shift of Louis XIV; the prostitute
with a pinched waist and great flowered sleeves of the Maison Doree.
She was as old as the first vice, as the first lust budding like a black
blossom in the morbidity of men successful, satiated. (258)

In the green mountain valley she is temptation personified. Though
not representative of rural schoolteachers, she has an occupation that
provides a satisfactory reason for bringing her into the book and also
explains why she is aware of life beyond the immediate area.

A sense of mortality permeates *Mountain Blood* and reinforces the
religious element. Hergesheimer achieves this largely not only by the
deaths of Pompey, Clare, Lettice, and Gordon. but also by a photograph of the deceased Mrs. Hollidew in her casket as a sort of *memento
mori* intermittently recurring. This device seems legitimate because
the practice of displaying such photographs has been common in
some parts of the nation, but the reader questions the shadow of doom
more than once said to appear near Lettice and to prophesy her death.
This feeling of mortality presumably stems from the author's life at
Woodnest, but it differs from the religious views he learned there.
In his childhood and youth he learned of a Day of Judgment and
eternal reward, but in the novel he saw life as leading only to "inevitable, blind termination" (240).

When Hergesheimer ventured that *Mountain Blood* was his only
novel that his grandfather might have approved of, he probably had
in mind the basic conception that avarice and other evils are punished
by death, making the book what he characterized as "an absolutely
Presbyterian performance."[12] The fact is, though, that organized religion receives negative rather than neutral treatment. The revival
meeting includes liquor as well as spirituality. The well-fed Universalist minister appears better suited to paternity than pastoral work,

the Roman Catholic priest seems a recluse, and the Methodists and the Presbyterians are represented principally by the money-hungry Pompey and Valentine. The positive aspect of the various groups' work remains unmentioned. Inasmuch as there appears no need for this treatment, Hergesheimer's negative depiction may be an indication of revolt against the religion of Woodnest. The reader also notes that *The Lay Anthony* ends with Tony's receiving the $47,000 after Eliza is dead; and in *Mountain Blood* Gordon learns just before he dies that a bank's coming to Greenstream will take the valley people out of the money-lenders' grasp. Such ironies suggest indifference or cruelty rather than benevolence in the universe.

These episodic apprentice works did not sell well (only 900 copies of *The Lay Anthony*), but they were appreciated by a few. Mitchell Kennerley's chief reader (Alfred A. Knopf) was enthusiastic about the typescript of *Mountain Blood* when he saw it in 1914. The regionalism probably was responsible for the encomiums from friends such as Mencken and Cabell, the latter as an example of the "beauty" of atonement, just as *The Lay Anthony* had concerned the "beauty" of chastity.[13] There were favorable reviews in respected periodicals such as the *Times* of London, *Nation*, and the *New York Times*.[14] In a letter to Mrs. John Boogher written 11 August 1919 about *The Lay Anthony*, Hergesheimer said, "There were some very beautiful reviews, it got me an entire willingness on the part of publishers to take whatever I might do. . . ." Though clearly minor, *The Lay Anthony* and *Mountain Blood* served as valuable preparation for the succeeding novels of greater worth, and, stylistically, the mannerisms prominent in the author's later work have their beginnings here.

Chapter Three

The Three Black Pennys

Encouraged by his two published novels and several *Saturday Evening Post* stories and living in the security of the Dower House, Hergesheimer wrote as he wished to write. Accordingly, he told a story combining his aestheticism and antiquarian interest, tinctured by the solid religious training of Woodnest. He later told Cabell that he sought to acheve an elusive quality;[1] and to Sinclair Lewis, he cited a line which for him epitomized the book: "Slag and metal and ruffled muslin, roman candles and stars."[2] These somewhat ambiguous statements are only partially clarified by his statement in the introduction to the 1930 edition that he had attempted to create "a spectacle of moving beauty," the characters being no more important to him than individual musical notes are to the theme:

What I meant in 1917 by a spectacle of moving beauty I could not have described. It was, I suppose, the inescapable fate of the human race. Collectively. A hard gained courage and loveliness consigned, like the vilest faults, to the same eternal blackness. I saw a beauty, the beauty of order, in the progress of the cause and effect I have mentioned. In, shortly, logic. Logic rather than justice. I was, even then, unable to discover the signs of any dependable justice. Either in the world I knew or the reported insubstantial worlds of the future. Howat Penny committed a fault—it was the premise of *The Three Black Pennys* that Howat's act constituted a fault—and, in another age, he paid with great exactness for it.[3]

The last sentence closely resembles a biblical passage the author presumably heard early in life, both at home and at church, in which the Lord says that he is "a jealous God, visiting the iniquity of the fathers upon the children unto the third and fourth generation of them that hate" Him (Exodus 20:5). In Hergesheimer's agnostic adulthood a *sin* has become a *fault*, and by a sort of secular doctrine of inherited guilt, Howat pays for his adultery through his descendants.

22

To fulfill this premise, the author uses an important scientific idea he had first mentioned in *The Lay Anthony*—Mendelian law, which he here applies to human beings.

A visit to a steel mill stimulated Hergesheimer's imagination so much that he wrote this novel and also "Steel," which ran in the *Saturday Evening Post*. To prepare himself, he spent several weeks laboring in a mill; and he employed help in his research into iron and steel from blooms to blast furnaces. Armed with a mass of accurate detail, he wrote the first draft in seventy-two days, beginning a pattern he followed in novels about the American past—careful research for exact details followed by rapid writing. The book's faults rarely were ones of fact.

What is a "black Penny"? As Gilbert Penny explained the term, the family, "some hundreds of years back, acquired a strong Welsh strain. I take it you are familiar with the Welsh—a solitary-living dark lot. Unamenable to influence, reflect their country, I suppose; but lovers of music. . . . Opposition's their breath" (39–40). Gilbert then pointed out that this inheritance appeared solidly in one person every two to four generations. To fit the recurrence of the recessive genetic strain in the Penny family, Hergesheimer took the tripartite structure of *Mountain Blood* and created a triptych which gives balance and allows a time span of 167 years.

Mosaic Law

The three parts into which the book is divided are titled "The Furnace," "The Forge," and "The Metal." Each section is built around a black Penny—Howat, Jasper, and Howat II, respectively. The first is a young man, the second is middle-aged, and the third is elderly. The progressive lives depict black Pennys from vigorous youth through troubled maturity to weakened old age and death.

"The Furnace." Howat, the dark-complexioned, twenty-five-year-old son of Gilbert, was the first "black penny" since the ancestor who died as a heretic in Queen Mary's day. As a child he was not amenable to discipline, and as an adult he is so contemptuous of the servility of most people that he complains to his mother that "there is something unendurable in men herding like cattle, protecting their fat with warning boards and fences" (7–8). He has never fallen in love because he regards it as a trap which leads people into animal-like breeding. As the son of the part-owner of Shadrach Furnace and

Myrtle Forge, Howat has had an opportunity to learn the iron business or to indulge in pastimes. He chooses the latter, particularly hunting.

As the book opens, Howat is returning hungry from a day's vain hunt. Nearing Shadrach Furnace, he sees geese flying overhead but does not try to fire his gun because of its faulty flint. He consorts somewhat with the flaming-haired Fanny Gilkan at the foundry, goes on an overnight hunt with her, and then goes to his home nine miles away at Myrtle Forge. There he finds Abner Forsythe, part-owner of Shadrach; his son David just returned from metallurgical study in England; Felix Winscombe, an elderly English diplomat; and the young Mrs. Winscombe who represents the licentiousness of a Court in which she has had lovers since age fourteen. Howat's sister Caroline wants David for herself, despite the common expectation that he will marry the other sister, the pretty Myrtle. When Felix is gone on a trip, Howat falls in love with Ludowika Winscombe and commits adultery with her. Caroline wins David; and when Felix returns ill and dies, Ludowika realizes her future lies with America and Howat, who will learn the iron business and succeed his father.

"The Forge."   The black Penny strain reappears in Ludowika's and Howat's great-grandson, Jasper. The vigorous, proud, and able owner of many furnaces and foundries, he married Phebe, a religious fanatic; but as a widower he now lives with his mother and aunt at Myrtle Forge. A few years earlier, though, he had made a liaison with Essie Scofield, a pretty but common woman by whom he has had a child, Eunice.

We meet the middle-aged Jasper at Myrtle Forge on a February day as he watches his workers chopping ice to free the water flow. The slow mending of his broken arm reminds him that though he is in his early forties, he inevitably will begin his decline in a few years. He has spent his youth in "an incomprehensible revolt" (142) and his adulthood in headstrong activity as a black Penny. Like Howat, he is dark-complexioned and has upsloping eyebrows; he has tramped off into the woods to escape the confining walls at home; and like Howat, he has committed adultery, but this time it is the man who is married rather than the woman. In his reaction against the other-worldliness and religious fanaticism of Phebe, Jasper has turned to the vivacious voluptuousness of Essie; but after a time the lovers have drifted apart. Now Jasper remembers the child and decides to find

her. In his efforts to get control of Eunice, Jasper turns to his relative
Stephen Jannan for legal advice. Jasper wins this battle but cannot
persuade Susan Brundon, a saintly schoolteacher, to marry him while
Essie is alive.

"The Metal." After Essie dies, Susan and Jasper marry and
have one son, who becomes the father of the third black Penny, the
second Howat. In his old age Howat has returned to Shadrach to live
after devoting his adult life to the enjoyment of music. Now with his
monocle he reads his scrapbooks of opera's great days and remembers
conductors, composers, and star performers such as Patti from the
nineteenth century. Rather frequently he is visited by his cousin
Mariana Jannan, a spirited society girl, with whom he gets along
well. She surprises him, however, when she brings as guests her relative
Eliza Jannan and James Polder, a descendant of Eunice Scofield, later
Penny. To the proud, effete Howat, Eliza is dangerously modern and
James is outside family acceptance.

Howat is the Penny line enfeebled, and he is the end of the Penny
name but not male inheritance, for that continues in James Polder.
The blackness becomes extinct, for only the love of music mentioned
by Gilbert remains in Howat; and he marches to a conductor's baton,
not to a triphammer. In his thinking, he is paying in his sterile life for
part of Jasper's indebtedness, and he cannot accept the Polders as
social equals. At Shadrach he and James have tense and uneasy words,
for the proud, ambitious young man is aware of the old scandal. After
Eliza and Polder depart, Mariana tells Howat that she loves James
but cannot make up her mind to marry him because she is torn between her love for him and her dislike for his lack of culture. To
help her decide, she accepts a dinner invitation to the Byron Polder
home for Howat and herself.

The dinner accentuates the social differences between the Polders
and their guests. It leads to James's marriage to an actress, and then
over some months both Mariana and Howat accept James for his
honesty and virility. Howat eventually comes to think that Jasper's
liaison has not weakened the ability of his grandson. When the
actress leaves James, Mariana moves in with him. Disliking departures
from established mores, Howat recognizes in Mariana's adulterous
living a defiant act like that of the first Howat; but he views the action
as one in a procession of lives, the fate of humanity. The old man
declines steadily until he is on his deathbed, and Mariana comes to

comfort him in his final illness. As he dies, he looks out the window
and sees geese flying overhead.

Analysis and Estimate

In *The Three Black Pennys*, the first full flowering of his talent,
Hergesheimer achieved a great advance over his first novels. He
broadened the book with subplots, included more of his own philosophy of life, and brought in the nostalgic lure of the past. He evoked
pictures of bygone years in a way that created a sweet melancholy
characterizing much of his future work.

Throughout the novel runs a sense of time's fleeting and of life's
transience. Hergesheimer suggests the passage of time by the altered
customs, clothing, and manners of the three periods, the shift from
iron to steel, and the successive generations of Pennys. Most effective
is the triphammer which beats out a chronometric message as well
as forged metal; it runs through the story from the days of the first
Howat to the memory of it by the second. The passing generations
remind one of Arnold Bennett's *The Old Wives' Tale*, though Hergesheimer's are not continuous. They presumably are to be like the
Endless Mountains that Gilbert Penny refers to or like the second
Howat's vision of a river flowing by, one in which he saw Mariana
engulfed in time and biology drifting along in the current. As generations succeed one another, Hergesheimer raises the question of
individual responsibility by a tantalizing suggestion of predestination
(177); but he does not pursue an idea that might absolve the first
Howat of his guilt. It is the indifferent consignment of mankind to
oblivion that lends an undertone of sadness and pity to the book.

Hergesheimer achieves a unity consisting not only in the black
Pennys and the ever-present elegiac mood but also in the recurring
beat of the triphammer which reminds the reader continuously of
iron and steel. Shadrach and Myrtle Forge run like a thread from
beginning to end. The rain on the roof when Howat and Ludowika
committed adultery is echoed in the elderly Howat's illusion of rain
on the roof. The note from Ludowika to Howat reappears in the
third part when it drops out of the old forgebook, which is mentioned in all three sections; and Mariana's protest against following
the rules of the card game reminds one of the unconventional Howat
of 1740. "The old fault," as the second Howat terms it, is present in
all three parts of the novel: adultery between Howat and Ludowika,

Jasper and Essie, and Mariana and James. Though not parallel in all respects, the Caroline-David relationship displays feminine determination similar to that of Mariana-James. There is also a necklace that came from Mrs. Gilbert Penny down through the years to Mariana. The steady flow of generations, which was the great interest of Hergesheimer, permeates the entire book and lends a feeling of continuity, the idea of the "endless" alluded to by the first Howat. And the author creates a roundedness by opening and closing with flying geese silhouetted against the sky, though, ironically, he later asserted that the pairing was accidental.[4]

The style Hergesheimer used in *The Three Black Pennys* is that which many readers associate with him. The opening of the novel is typical of it and of the nature descriptions: "A twilight like blue dust shifted into the fold of the thickly wooded hills. It was early October, but a crisping frost had already stamped the maple trees with gold, the Spanish oaks were hung with patches of wine red, the sumac was brilliant in the darkening underbrush. A pattern of wild geese, flying low and unconcerned above the hills, wavered against the serene, ashen evening" (3). In this passage one sees the bold contrasts Hergesheimer had come to use in his visual sensuous appeal. Added to the vivid description are names such as Appletofft and Kingsfrere which lend an exotic note. "Polder," though, might have been included because of its suggestive meaning: "reclaimed land." All in all, the style seems aimed at producing an impression rather than thought.

There are occasional weaknesses in the book. Sometimes an awkward sentence occurs, as "The dog maintained stridulous barking; and James Polder carried her, in an ecsatsy [*sic*] of snarling ill-temper, out" (352). There are mistakes such as dangling constructions, use of the superlative for the comparative (Caroline as the "oldest" of two), and faulty verbs ("Howat raised up slowly"). Such errors, though infrequent, reflect the author's lack of a sound education.

But the errors drew less censure than some of the mannerisms which had become entrenched in his novels. The conjunction of pronoun and proper noun such as "He, Howat" (291) and "He, Howat Penny" (377) occurs occasionally. The use of the full name rather than the given or last one is prominent again; as a result, we see Jasper Penny, Essie Scofield, James Polder, and Howat Penny repeatedly. Also, there sometimes are too many commas when the author seeks a particular effect: "It had been an error: yet there had been, within him, no choice, no intimation of a different, more desirable, consummation" (281). The last phrase illustrates a distinctive stylistic trait that appeared at times in the apprentice novels but becomes full-blown here and irritated Cabell so much that he parodied it and other mannerisms in a letter to Burton Rascoe: "There is no necessity for talk, explanations, but he, Hergesheimer, after writing this book, this novel, about Howat Penny and what he, Howat, bequeathed, left his descendants, should be watched, observed—something too much of this appositional style I notice, and reproduce for your benefit."[5]

A key to this book lies in the author's being an aesthete with some training in art. Evidence can be found from beginning to end in his attention to how he stated his ideas and in the predominance of visual imagery; Hergesheimer saw the scenes as a painter would, being affected most by Velasquez and Degas. In the dedication to Dorothy's cousin John Hemphill, for example, we find reference to "June nights on the porch, with the foliage of the willow tree powdered against the stars; the white-panelled hearth of the yellow room in smouldering winter dusks; dinner with the candles wavering in tepid April airs; and the blue envelopment of late September noons." The descriptive passages customarily contain an amplitude of detail, often being complete rather than selective.

Perhaps the most distinctive mark of the aestheticism, though, is Hergesheimer's emphasis on decor. A table at Stephen Jannan's, for instance, is pictured in ornate detail: "A long table was burdened with elaborate pagodas of spun barley sugar topped with sprigs of orange blossoms, the moulded creams of a Charlotte Polonaise, champagne jelly valanced with lemon peel, pyramids of glazed fruits on lacquered plates; with faintly iridescent Belleek and fluted glass and ormolu; and, everywhere, the pale multitudinous flames of candles and the fuller radiance of astral lamps hung with lustres" (167). The aestheticism runs throughout the book but is most pronounced in the third part, in which Howat recalls opera seasons and performances of the past. It is not dissociated from morality, however, as it would be in George Moore; and the early religious training is still present in a modified form. Although Hergesheimer changes the term *sin* to *fault* and speaks of *logic*, he still means punishment for wrongdoing.

In *The Three Black Pennys* Hergesheimer began a method of

characterization he followed in most of his succeeding volumes. He took pride in his understanding of women, even comparing himself to Turgenev in his achievement;[6] and indeed critics from the Columbia University professor Carl Van Doren[7] to Clifton Fadiman[8] usually regarded his female portraits as his greatest strength. The English writer J. B. Priestley observed that the women did not have an existence independent of the men,[9] and Cabell called them "troublingly ornamental odalisques" who usually were "avocational interests."[10] Hergesheimer wanted what he called *vitality* most of all, and he threw his creations into distinct relief by contrasting them. The plain, strong-willed Caroline, for instance, is the opposite of the pretty and gentle Myrtle; and the effete, elderly, and cultured second Howat is the opposite of the powerful, young, uncultured James. Hergesheimer placed the ladies into a more restricted pattern than the men because he saw them that way—"delicate and charming in cambric and chiffon, tender and faithful and passionate (xv). In embryonic form Eliza in *The Lay Anthony* and Lettice in *Mountain Blood* fit this description, but they died young. It is Ludowika who serves as the prototype for a long succession of main female characters, including Mariana. Curiously, Hergesheimer made these ladies distinctive not always by physical appearance but by vitality and determination.

The first Howat also serves as a prototype, but there is less standardization among the men than the women. While the latter represented universal feminine attributes, the male protagonists were endowed with the qualities the author thought he himself lacked—courage, independence, vigor, and strength. The first Howat, Jasper, and James fit well his observation to Mrs. C. L. Brown that "Rude and primitive and quite desperate gentlemen seem to attract me. . . ." (5 May 1926). These characters tend to remain static; oddly, though, it is the second Howat who shows some character development by growing from his snobbish rejection of James Polder to acceptance of the young man and admiration for the strengths and genuineness he possessed.

The "blackness" of the Pennys is used in two senses—complexion and characteristics. They were all dark, but the physical attribute of sloping eyebrows inherited from Howat and Ludowika seems incidental, and the characteristics are more important. The first Howat and Jasper had pride, intractability, and scorn of conventions; and the second Howat, because of the weakening of the strain, had only pride and the love of music. Though the men differed thus, the author intends an identification of the three:

It was at once himself and that other Howat, yes, and Jasper. All three unremarkably merged into one. And the acts of the first, a dark young man with an erect, impatient carriage, a countenance and gaze of vigorous scorn, accumulated in a later figure, hardly less upright, slender, but touched with grey—a man in the middle of life. He paid with an anguished spirit for what had taken place; and at last an old man lingered with empty hands, the husk of a passion that had burned out all vitality. (406–7)

Applying Mendelian law to the Pennys and suggesting the power of inheritance in James's fondness for orange juice and gin after the manner of Essie, Hergesheimer creates a sense of a powerful inherited biological base to character. Strangely for Hergesheimer, Mariana's adulterous living with James seems to portend a renewal in the family strength, so that the Penny pride and industrial drive will live on, though the name has become extinct in this branch of the family.

Ordinarily humor has not been attributed to Hergesheimer; however, two events in this novel have comic overtones: the wedding and the dinner at the Polders'. In these episodes the author skillfully juxtaposes the monocled Howat's love of opera and his superior social status with the plebeian life and tastes of the Byron Polder family. At the wedding the banging of the steam radiators provides a cacophonous accompaniment to the ceremony, lending an ironically appropriate noise to an iron and steel man's nuptials and portending a stormy marriage. The second event, more fully described, is unusual in the author's novels, for it is a realistic modern picture in the vein of Sinclair Lewis which reminds the reader of a dinner in *Babbitt* a few years later. Determined to be correctly obnoxious, Howat dresses formally for dinner at the Polders', one result of which is a voice heard on his and Mariana's arrival: " 'I told you,' it said violently, '. . . dress suit' " (312). Mrs. Polder is nervous, the father, Byron, is boorishly condescending, James is worried, his sister Isabella is interested in the social aspects, and his sister Kate radiates confident beauty. Mrs. Polder comments that his monocle is like that of the prominent actor George Arliss. There is a discussion of Eliza Jannan's being arrested and speculation on how it would be if Isabella Polder were. " 'Imagine Isabella!' Jim Polder exploded. 'It's quite the thing,' that individual asserted. 'Isabella,' her mother declared, 'it is twenty-five past seven. I wish you'd go out and see where dinner is.' She rose with an expression of mingled surprise and pain. 'Really, mother,' she said, 'that is an extraordinary request.' Her brother snorted. There was a sudden muffled clamour of chimes from below, and Mrs. Polder gave a sigh of relief. 'I didn't want it spoiled,' she explained, descending; 'Jim would be wild after all his eagerness to have things nice' " (316). After dinner Mrs. Polder suggests music.

"My son says you are very fond of good music," she addressed Howat Penny. "I can tell you it is a lovely taste. We have the prettiest records that come. Isabella, put on *Hark, Hark, the Lark*." She obediently rose, and, revolving the handle of the talking machine, fixed the grooved, rubber disk and needle. Howat listened with a stony countenance to the ensuing strains. Such instruments were his particular detestation. Mrs. Polder waved her hand dreamily. "Now," she said, "the *Sextette*, and *The End of a Perfect Day*. No, Mr. Penny would like to hear *Salome*, I'm sure, with all those cymbals and creepy Eastern tunes." (318)

After condescending remarks from Byron Polder, a record featuring banjos drowns all conversation. Immediately after, the bell rings, and the actress Harriet de Barry bursts in. All in all, the aristocratic Howat is pleased with the boorish affair because he thinks the contrast between it and those in the proper social world will cause Mariana to reject James. Inasmuch as the humor consists largely in the contrast between social levels, Howat's point of view is ideal for these comic and satiric episodes. The uncharacteristic humor may have been stimulated by Sinclair Lewis, for it was during this period that he and Hergesheimer corresponded and visited.

Because his first two novels had not paid the publisher's expenses, Hergesheimer was overjoyed to learn that the first edition of his third novel had sold out in a week.[11] Not only did the public buy the book but the reviewers and friends generally were complimentary and specified particular points for praise. Among such were the technique of telling the story, cited by the *New Republic*,[12] and the brooding tone, mentioned by H. W. Boynton in *Bookman*.[13] Of the friends, Lewis offered the most detailed evaluation in a letter. Differing with Vernon Louis Parrington, who later thought "the first episode [was] Hergesheimer at his best,"[14] Lewis regarded the first part as too much like Pepys and containing too much material, but he found the characters real and the dinner at the Polders' superb (3 November [1917]).

Hergesheimer was happy with the generally favorable attention, because, as he wrote to Mencken, he was uneasy about his first novel after two years of the *Saturday Evening Post* (13 August 1917).

The Three Black Pennys is one of the best of the few aesthetic novels in the United States. It did not set a trend for others, but it was significant for the author because it was the first of several books about the past, his initial popular success, and the first American novel published by Knopf. It came at a time without many major novels, and it proved that the nation had a past which could be used even without the great age that Hawthorne and Henry James desired. It also, as Hergesheimer wrote to John Hemphill (7 June 1924), led to an agreement to give Hergesheimer the right of approving the scenario, the location, the cast, and the final production of a prospective movie. This extraordinary policy arose from his frustration with the filming of *Tol'able David*, the hit starring Richard Barthelmess.[15] The popular new book led to status among authors with whom Hergesheimer could now fraternize as an established figure. In England as well he became recognized as an important personage. When W. L. George, critic, wrote an article on Hergesheimer for the London *Bookman* in 1920, he stated that Hergesheimer was the only young American to make a reputation on his first appearance in England (as he did with the publication of *The Three Black Pennys*) and that in America and in Europe the only writer suitable for comparison was Joseph Conrad.[16] For the five-year period begun with *The Three Black Pennys*, Hergesheimer and his aestheticism remained highly rated in the American and British literary world.

Chapter Four
Java Head

In *Java Head*, generally rated his best book, Hergesheimer discarded entirely the moral base of *Mountain Blood* and *The Three Black Pennys* and created a story aimed at the aesthetic sense. In doing this, he placed the events in the summer of 1847 in declining Salem, Massachusetts, made opium the cause of most action, and assumed that life in the Orient destroyed Westerners, and life in the Occident destroyed Orientals.[1] As he wrote to Captain Arthur H. Clark, the marriage of a Salem ship captain to a Manchu was bound to produce "disastrous results" (15 April 1918).

The book takes its title from the name the retired sea captain Jeremy Ammidon gave his house to signify safety at the end of a long voyage. The family includes Jeremy, his son William and his buxom wife Rhoda, their four sturdy daughters (Sidsall, Camilla, Janet, and Laurel), and the younger son, Gerrit. William manages the affairs of the firm of Ammidon, Ammidon, and Saltonstone on land; and Gerrit, preferring the sea, captains the *Nautilus*, one of the ships. Contrasted with this prosperous firm is that of the Dunsacks, who earn meager returns from the West Indies trade. The religious fanatic Barzil dominates the family, which includes the son, Edward, an opium addict just returned from China; the daughter, Kate; and Nettie Vollar, Kate's illegitimate daughter. In addition to the two families is Roger Brevard, an educated marine insurance salesman. A few residents of Salem occasionally appear, but the Ammidon and Dunsack families and Gerrit's Manchu bride, Taou Yuen (Peach Garden), are at the center of the story.

East and West

The plot of *Java Head* is relatively simple, but the development is complex, largely because Hergesheimer tells the story in ten chapters, using the following successive points of view: Laurel, Jeremy,

Rhoda, Gerrit, Edward, Sidsall, Nettie, Gerrit, Taou Yuen, and Roger Brevard. The action begins in late May 1847, when Laurel Ammidon has just turned eleven and begins to abandon her childish transformation of furniture into persons. She knows the family is intensely concerned over her uncle Gerrit, seven months overdue from a trip to the Orient. She goes for walks with her heavy, florid grandfather, Jeremy, and enjoys the treats he buys for her. In succeeding chapters we see anxiety over Gerrit build up until one day he returns. In his cargo he has Edward Dunsack's trunk, which he has transported as a favor and which unknown to him contains opium. Then we see the family's and town's astonishment when Gerrit brings his Manchu bride home from the ship. Independent and ready to disregard public opinion, Gerrit insists on taking her to church, where she is subjected to the boorish stares of the townspeople. As weeks pass, Taou Yuen is uncomfortable in Salem, Edward becomes infatuated with her, and Gerrit is subjected to the attractions of Nettie, a former friend, who is still interested in him. Nettie is befriended by the Ammidons at the Fourth of July celebration, and her uncle Edward insists to her that Gerrit owes her something because of an earlier friendship. Jeremy dies from the shock of learning that William has been trafficking in opium. When President Polk visits, Nettie is injured in the crush. Curious about Gerrit's former friend, Taou Yuen visits her, Edward tries to put his hands on the Manchu, and she swallows Nettie's medicinal opium to kill herself and remain unsullied. A brief time after the funeral Gerrit and Nettie are married and depart on the *Nautilus*. Gerrit has left the firm of Ammidon, Ammidon, and Saltonstone and taken over the affairs of the Dunsacks. Roger Brevard, who unsuccessfully courted the young Sidsall Ammidon, remains to observe and symbolize the decay of Salem.

Genesis and Development

For *Java Head* we fortunately have fuller knowledge of the genesis and development than of the other novels by the author. We do not know why Hergesheimer turned to a seaport for his fourth novel, but a number of factors may have influenced him. He had sailed down the coast on the yacht *Wabun*, he had visited New England, and he may have read his father's sea books. Whatever it was that sparked his initial interest, he characteristically began with a picture—his "vision of a nonconformist Salem shipmaster in the restricted area of the American hong at Canton, attended by servants in silk, a servant to bear his parasol, the servant who carried a lacquered stool, a servant with the lime leaves and betel nuts he chewed held in a brocade bag."[2]

After he had determined to write a novel suggested by the mental picture, Hergesheimer began extensive research, as he had for *The Three Black Pennys*. He visited Salem, read ninety-five books, took forty thousand words of notes, and wrote the first draft of the book in two months in the spring of 1918.[3] Then came the revision after expert advice, printing in the *Saturday Evening Post* from 5 October to 9 November 1918, and finally publication by Knopf on 28 December 1918. It was the author's second novel about the American past and his second written under the influence of the Dower House.

From the research he probably took the sailor's chanteys, such as

"The times are hard and wages low,
　　Oh, leave her, Johnny, leave her.
I guess it's time for us to go,
　　Oh, leave her, Johnny, leave her.
I thought I heard the old man say,
　　Oh leave her, Johnny, leave her.
To-morrow we will get our pay
　. . . . . leave her."[4]

Not satisfied with merely his own knowledge, he had his typescript checked by authorities: the Peabody Museum; Captain Arthur H. Clark, maritime expert; and Dr. and Mrs. Isaac T. Headland, longtime residents of China. We do not have any changes in historical facts which may have been suggested by the Peabody Museum, but we do have some record of the alterations on navigation suggested by Captain Clark and on Chinese life and customs by Dr. and Mrs. Headland. Captain Clark, not restricting himself to sailing matters, objected to a formality or stiffness, advised a careful rewriting, and set up an appointment for discussion of the nautical aspects of the book, in which he found a "great many inaccuracies" (18 April 1918). Thirteen days later Clark wrote that he had made several corrections and had rewritten a number of scenes but that much work remained (1 May 1918). On 6 May he said that he had twenty-two pages of memoranda and rewriting to discuss. Presumably Hergesheimer adopted many of Clark's suggestions, for the author later acknowledged being saved from many errors by the captain's advice.[5]

Because the letter from Mrs. Headland still exists, we can see specific changes recommended and adopted. On 13 April 1918 Hergesheimer seems to have sent the manuscript to the Headlands requesting advice about Taou Yuen. In her long, detailed reply Mrs. Headland mentioned first that there would be no objection to having a Manchu lady ordering her life according to Tao, although she had never known one to do so. The remarriage she found more difficult, but she suggested a way to solve the problem. A necromancer could tell the father-in-law of the widowed Taou Yuen that his family's misfortunes were owing to her presence; and he, liking his daughter-in-law, could tell Gerrit, who could see her in a garden. She then would see him and fall in love, and after the marriage he could take her away forever. She would be a clever girl who had read foreign books. On clothes, Mrs. Headland objected that the ones in the typescript apparently belonged to actors because Taou Yuen's would be different: "No description could give an adequate idea to a foreigner of the beauty and loveliness of garments I have seen Manchu ladies wear. The loveliest shades of pinks, greens, blues, yellows—every shade indeed—in brocaded satin embroidered with the most exquisite flowers—wisteria, chrysanthemums, peonies, roses, cherry blossoms, butterflies; all kinds of flowers; but the dragons are reserved for the princes and their wives and the Emperor and Empresses." Mrs. Headland said that in the typescript the only indication she found of Jeremy's death was a tablet and implied that his decease should have been noted earlier. She also mentioned the three religions, the favor the ladies showed Kuan Yin pu tze, the Goddess of Mercy, and the mourning garment of white sackcloth worn for 100 days and dark clothing for three years. A comparison of the letter with the text reveals that Hergesheimer adopted almost all of Mrs. Headland's points, deviating mainly in having a gravestone for Taou Yuen, probably because she was buried in Massachusetts after a Christian service. The use of Mrs. Headland's information demonstrates how at this time the author built his aesthetic novel on a solid factual base.

Analysis and Estimate

Aestheticism and the multiple point of view are distinguishing marks of *Java Head*. Its aestheticism is the primary fact about it as a novel. Hergesheimer was not seeking to construct a conventional story of his day but first to satisfy his own artistic preferences and then appeal to the few of like mind, such as Cabell (15 June 1918), who would appreciate the exotic touch of the proverb from the Taoist Chwang-tze on the title page: "It is only the path of pure simplicity which guards and preserves the spirit." During these years he was downplaying plot and character, while he emphasized vivid, sensuous accounts of surface life, as in Salem. Again he appeals to a feeling for the shape and sound of words, as in his favorites "ormolu" and "emerald," or in flower names such as "Ashton Towns," "jargonelles," and "white Chasselas," or in listing money from East India, China, Cochin China, Japan, Singapore, Java, Siam, and other Oriental places. Now and then he combines the olfactory and visual senses, particularly in the lilacs whose odor wafts through the pages; or he describes the cargo of "heavy plaited mats of cassia with a delicate scent, . . . bags with sharp conflicting odors, baled silks and half chests of tea wrapped in bamboos and matting painted with the ship's name, *Rose and Rosalie*" (161–62). More strikingly yet, he described Taou Yuen in church: "Fretted sandalwood bracelets dropped over her hands, and miniature dragon flies [*sic*] quivered on the gold wire of her earrings; the sharp perfumes of the East drifted out and mingled with the Western scents of extracts and powders. He only saw that she was politely chewing betel nut" (96). Such sensory detail seems to exist for its own sake as much as to set off the Manchu from the drab townspeople.

In his visual appeal Hergesheimer has no use for the pastels but prefers bright colors and strong contrasts. Sometimes the description is the simple one of golden sails in the sunset as the *Nautilus* slips into the harbor; at others it is colorful scenes of various military organizations drilling in preparation for July Fourth, of Nettie with her black curls restrained by a scarlet shawl as she hurries to the parade, of a palanquin, or of band men who wear scarlet uniforms and tall hats with chin straps.

One of the most prominent passages aimed at the eye is that describing Taou Yuen's costume. It exemplifies the type of verbal painting in which the author later said he used details like colors on his palette:[6]

Never before had Rhoda seen such lovely clothes: A long gown with wide sleeves of blue-black satin, embroidered in peach-colored flower petals and innumerable minute sapphire and orange butterflies, a short sleeveless jacket of sage green caught with looped red jade buttons and threaded with silver and indigo high-soled slippers crusted and tasseled with pearls. Her hair rose from the back in a smooth burnished loop. There were long pins of pink jade carved into blossoms, a quivering decoration of paper-thin gold leaves with moonstones in glistening drops, and a band of coral lotus buds. Pierced stone bracelets hung about her delicate wrists, fretted crystal balls swung from the lobes of her ears; and clasped on the ends of several fingers were long pointed filagrees [*sic*] of ivory. (74–75)

This description, which recalls Mrs. Headland's advice, was superior enough of its kind to draw Cabell's praise for the " 'rendering' of the surface and look of things" (6 January 1919).

Even more characteristic of Hergesheimer is decor, which he had begun to emphasize in *The Three Black Pennys*. The reader feels the aesthetic sensitivity of Hergesheimer in passages such as the one telling of Gerrit's going to the drawing room: "The long glass doors to the garden were open, and the interior was filled with the scent of lilacs. The room itself had always reminded him of them—it was pale in color, cool gilt and lavender brocade and white panels. Nothing had been moved or changed: the inlaid cylinder fall desk with its garlands of painted flowers on the light waxed wood stood at the left, the pole screen with the embroidered bouquet was before the fire blind, the girandoles, scrolled in ormolu and hung with crystal lusters, held the shimmer of golden reflections on the walls" (80). Carefully detailed descriptions such as this support Hergesheimer's frequent comment to Van Vechten that he cared more for decors than for people.[7] Indeed, the fondness for ornate decor and the small interest in character fit Hergesheimer's aesthetic sensibilities perfectly.

The author extended the experimentation with a multiple point of view begun in *The Three Black Pennys* and fourteen years later effectively continued in *The Limestone Tree*. In *Java Head*, unlike the others, he covers a time span of a few months rather than several generations. Following one person and then another as they are involved with the central story gives a clearer picture of them, it lends substance to a rather thin plot, it facilitates creating anxiety about the overdue Gerrit, and it avoids developing any one character thoroughly, a task the author repeatedly objected to because, he said, " 'I hate individuals. . . . I study what moves people without seeing the individuals at all.' "[8] With the multiple point of view, some distinctive aspects of *Java Head* the reader perceives are the treatment of religions, the contrast between old and new, and the assumption of a necessary tragedy in an East-West marriage. Revelatory of the author rather than the characters is the treatment of religions. *Mountain Blood* portrayed the wages of sin, though the individual church groups were not treated favorably; and *The Three Black Pennys* incorporated a secularized Mosaic law; but *Java Head* seems more favorable toward Taoism, Confucianism, and Buddhism as they are exemplified in the life of Taou Yuen rather than toward Christianity. Nettie characterizes the uncharitable Salem women's attitude toward her as "Christian"; Hodie, the Methodist, appears to be a joyless fanatic; Jeremy, admirable Congregational patriarch though he is, swears copiously and angers quickly; and William, the Unitarian, clearly separates his religion from his practice by trafficking in opium. Barzil Dunsack, preaching a God of wrath without forgiveness or compassion, breaks Kate's spirit, ruins her life, and creates a dominant negative tone from the Old Testament, the source of his name. And the congregation at the Sunday service exudes bigotry rather than charity; the men obviously disapprove of Taou Yuen, a "heathen," and the curious women boorishly finger her clothes. Only the unorthodox Gerrit shows charity and understanding toward the views of others. Perhaps these facts are what Hergesheimer had in mind when he wrote to Mencken that the book was not a strong support to piety (5 April 1918).

Just as in *The Three Black Pennys*, there again is an undercurrent of sadness and a feeling of the impermanence of life; Jeremy and Taou Yuen die, the Ammidon firm is moving to Boston, and the influence of Jeremy and the honest old days is declining before men like William. The necessity for building clipper ships to meet competition is understandable, but William's involving the firm in the opium trade is mere greed; and it is the old, represented by Jeremy, that is killed by the immoral commerce. The novel opens joyously with Laurel, but it proceeds through unhappiness to the somber valedictory with Brevard.

The author's assumption that an East-West marriage necessarily would yield tragic results is questionable. As he rightly stated, opium is the main agent—not only does its being on a manifest kill Jeremy, but it ruins Edward Dunsack in the Orient; it leads to his threatening Taou Yuen in the Occident and is the means of suicide for her. Nevertheless, Hergesheimer's idea that the West was destroyed by the East and the East by the West seems unproven. That there were difficulties such as an unfriendly reception of Taou Yuen is true, and Brevard thought that America had killed Taou Yuen, but it was specifically the threatening Dunsack that caused the Manchu lady's suicide. Had he not menaced her, she presumably would have lived in the tropical home Gerrit planned.

About *Java Head*, the author wrote, "It is simpler, less formal, and I think has more the aroma of life,—I mean as opposed to the aroma of books."[9] In most respects it is indeed less complex than his preceding volumes and is written in a style that gave Hergesheimer some difficulty, as he confessed to Van Vechten. With no literary allusions and only one biblical reference, it avoids bookishness. Set beside the occasional decor, this simplified style forms a contrast which parallels that between Taou Yuen and the less sophisticated Salemites. It led to a greater simplicity in diction, as we can see in a passage from Nettie's chapter: "She wondered a little, her emotion subsiding, at the interest her uncle showed in her affairs. It wasn't like what else she had gathered of him; and she searched, but without success, for any hidden reason he might have. He actively blackened the name of Ammidon while he was lost in too great an indifference to be moved by any but extraordinary pressures. Everything left his mind, as her mother had said, almost immediately. Suddenly weary, she gave up all effort at understanding" (157). Along with the less bookish diction go fewer mannerisms and occasional mataphors, the best of which probably is, "A soul was nothing more than a twisting leaf in the wind of fate" (108). Sometimes the author falters in his word choice as in writing "inimicable" for "inimical," and "impracticable" for "impractical"; but in general the word selection is more satisfactory than in the preceding novels.

Though foreshadowing is competently handled, some other aspects are not, according to customary novel standards. We fear for Jeremy, for example, when we see his florid face and realize his advice is neither sought nor desired anymore. The multiple point of view is clever, but it interferes with focus in the ordinary sense. There is an inconsistency between the expressed attitude of the sailors toward having a lady on board and the ending. Rhoda warns that Taou Yuen cannot live on the *Nautilus* (89), and Gerrit himself reflects that the superstitious seamen would object to a wife aboard (196). Yet at the end Nettie and Gerrit depart on the ship.

In a letter to George Melford of Famous Players Laskey Corporation the author told how he saw the characters (28 September 1922).

He conceived of Taou Yuen and Nettie as opposites, and apparently he intended to treat the other main characters comparably. Taou Yuen, of course, is delineated most thoroughly of the women, not only by her actions but also by her appearance. Hergesheimer suggests her subtle, complex nature in passages such as the one first describing her toilet articles and exotic, ornate wooden chest and continuing, "On a familiar table was her pipe, wound in gilt wire, and the flowered satin tobacco case. An old coin was hanging at the head of the bed, a charm against evil spirits; and on a stand was the amethyst image of Kuan-Yin *pu tze*, the Goddess of Mercy" (84). Her austere beauty, complex personality, elegant clothing as well as her unfamiliar Oriental religious customs and her universal feminine nature make her a vividly etched figure. Nettie, using no cosmetics, appears as an unfortunate, complaining, simple, voluptuous woman. Other female figures who stand out are Laurel and Rhoda. The former is a delightful, innocent, vigorous girl who is attractive not only at the novel's opening but also later in her repetitions of Jeremy's language, such as nautical terms. Rhoda stands as the central stabilizing figure, one with sense, kindness, understanding, and courage. Her concern for Jeremy, Nettie, Taou Yuen, and Sidsall reveals her as a strong, motherly character who does what needs doing on all occasions.

The male characters are clearly depicted also. Jeremy, a kindly but testy old man, is a lovable creation whom Hergesheimer shows in the company of Laurel as an affectionate grandfather with slightly salty language and in the company of his sons as the outdated representative of Salem's great days. William, who quietly loves his father, is the picture of an opportunistic business man. Gerrit, whose shortness is suggested by his wearing a tall hat when he arrives and departs, finds loneliness on shore rather than at sea, because on land he sees human pettiness such as hypocrisy complicating life. A champion of the unfortunate, he prefers the orderly existence on the ocean with the regularity and exactitude of the sun, the breaking of waves, the storage of cargo, and the ship's response to the wind. He loves the challenge of the open water, where he is safe from the ossified corruption on land. Nevertheless, he seems less vivid than Edward, who reveals his nature by his mean thoughts as well as by his scoundrelly actions. Barzil Dunsack is the type that makes virtue unpleasant, and Brevard is a fitting representative of the port's sinking fortunes.

Java Head won both an audience among the discerning public and the respect of critics, though no credit in the family. Humorous though it may be, Hergesheimer's achievement was unappreciated by his relatives. According to him, they thought writing a novel was a simple or possibly fraudulent act;[10] and his mother, perhaps reflecting her work-oriented environment at Woodnest, referred to the book as *Jog Ahead*. In 1919 Van Doren wrote one of the fuller and more perceptive evaluations in *Saturday Review* (London).[11] He pointed out the resemblance to painting and eulogized the creation of atmosphere: "The tranquil leisure of the Salem houses, with their vines and their arbours, the broad sunny streets, sweet with the scent of lilac and magnolia, the wharves crowded with many coloured cargoes, the endless magic of the sea, of perilous voyages, of those who do their business in great waters, the secure common sense of the West, touched with something of the colour and inscrutability of the East, all this and more lives for us and holds us." For Van Doren though, the characters were sketches rather than fully developed persons; and minor characters such as Laurel and Jeremy were better done than other more important ones, such as Gerrit. Van Doren also calls the ending less than satisfactory.

On most points a modern critic would agree with him. The atmosphere is excellent, though we must grant a nonexistent presidential visit to Salem and allow an anachronistic shift of the Gold Rush to 1847. On characters, too, one concedes Van Doren's points because Gerrit is present but insubstantial. It should be remembered that Hergesheimer was not seeking to write a historical novel and was detached from his characters and that the lack of depth may arise from stressing the juxtaposition of opposites such as Taou Yuen-Nettie, Gerrit-Edward, and Jeremy-Barzil. Because the emphasis is on the opposing qualities, the characters tend to be clearly etched but not rounded. Yet Edward's low, mean, jealous thoughts of Gerrit are well done; and Taou Yuen's curiosity about Nettie humanizes her. The ending seems not to grow out of the preceding action. The early concern over Gerrit establishes him as the protagonist, whose fate should determine the nature of the story, and all signs point to an unhappy denouement, but Gerrit's marriage to Nettie provides an unexpectedly happy touch, diminished though it is by Taou Yuen's death. The fact that Roger Brevard ends the novel with his courting failure and bleak future seems appropriate, but he is a minor character. Readers are more likely to hold Edward responsi-

ble for the beauteous Manchu's death than the Occident or, more
specifically, America. Nevertheless, as Van Doren implies, Hergesheimer did create an aesthetically appealing set of pictures of Salem
in the summer of 1847 (what his English publisher Heinemann
called a "still life" [24 June 1919]).

Later several respected academic critics assessed *Java Head* from
the vantage point of some years, during which the author's reputation had declined steadily. In their brief comments Joseph Warren
Beach and Arthur Hobson Quinn termed the novel decorative rather
than dramatic and noted that atmosphere was the most important
element.[12] Parrington, who leaned toward a social emphasis, called
Java Head the author's best but sensed a questionable artistic sincerity;[13] and Walter Fuller Taylor saw the aesthetic standard and an
undefined deficiency.[14] Still later, in *Scholastic*, the eminent historian
Henry Steele Commager saw Salem as both plot and setting and
noted the author's power for evoking setting: "Joseph Hergesheimer
has always had a peculiar talent for evoking the appearance, the feeling, the very texture of places, and that talent is here highly developed. Few other novels carry us back so imaginatively to a time
and a society that is lost and now but a memory."[15] These evaluations
in general are discerning and accurate, but Parrington's doubt of
artistic sincerity is merely opinion, and Taylor's perception of a deficiency needs further examination.

Taylor's point appears to be what Cabell referred to in a letter
to Guy Holt: "It is good, but not Economic: in fact, I am astounded
to note how good it is, without ever attaining the whatever-it-is that
Hergesheimer's writing lacks. I don't know what this something is:
but in reading I desiderate it."[16] Because Cabell was a close literary
friend and a fellow aesthete, his censure deserves serious consider-
ation in any judgment of *Java Head*. At this time the two authors
were so friendly that Hergesheimer included in a letter to Cabell
a bit of doggerel beginning, "*Joe and Jim and none beside*," denoting
the exclusivity of the two aesthetes in their search for beauty. The
friendliness, however, did not mean the two authors agreed on all
literary matters. Cabell, who was well educated and even taught at
William and Mary College for a short time, approved the ending
but hinted to Hergesheimer that the novel was two-dimensional when
he called it "miraculously superficial" in a congratulatory letter (6
January 1919). To Hugh Walpole, Cabell was direct when he asked
the latter to "duly lecture [Hergesheimer] upon the unimportance

of externals"; and to prove a need for such he cited as an example that
Hergesheimer was excited by superficial "truths" such as the apparent
violet tint in a girl's blue eyes if she has red hair.[17] What Cabell,
Taylor, and others found a lack probably arose from Hergesheimer's
emphasis on verbal painting. The basic question, then, is whether
the book is to be taken on its own terms or not, since the author
sought only a gratifying picture rather than significance.[18] Hergesheimer accomplished very well what he set out to do, but most readers
expect meaning, more plot, and more fully developed main characters.

Chapter Five
Linda Condon

Hergesheimer did not pause after his success with *Java Head*. He was writing short stories and reviews even as the book was being published on 28 December 1918; and early in February he was well into *Linda Condon*,[1] his first contemporary novel since *Mountain Blood*. Though his radical experimentation with the multiple point of view had been successful, he chose to tell his new story from the single point of view in a conventional structure. Apparently he had long wished to develop a novel somewhat like the present one, as he reminded Van Vechten, to whom he dedicated it: "You well know, my dear Carl, for how long I have wanted to write the story of *Linda Condon*, that charming grave child with her straight black bang and vivid blue eyes, placed with her light-hearted mother in hotels of amazing adornment. Here, at last, it is. But—a thing, it seems, inevitable and which we forgot to discuss—Linda grew up. She lost the childhood that was my first concern and her story developed into the record of a sustained affair of the heart."[2] In a short time he completed his work, and the story appeared in *Everybody's Magazine* from May to December 1919, and as a book on 1 November of that year.

But *Linda Condon* includes more than Hergesheimer's interest in a ten-year-old girl who grew up; the theme is a combination of that and the author's fascination with beauty, art, and Neoplatonism. The book tells of a creative artist's growth and Linda's gradual comprehension of Neoplatonism. Apparently from his reading, Hergesheimer learned of the medieval Academy of Ficino and the concept of ascending types of beauty and love; and from it he received confirmation of an idea he already held—that of a spiritual relationship between the artist and his physical inspiration. This knowledge excited him so much that for a period, according to Rascoe, he was garrulous about Neoplatonism.[3]

In one sense, this novel is an artistic autobiography of the author.

45

He saw some parallels between Linda and himself: no education,
unsatisfactory early companions, and Linda's desire to understand
and assist Pleydon balances against Hergesheimer's attempt to express
the highest beauty, while knowing that "the body [labored] far behind
the spirit."[4] The book establishes his relationship to literature,[5] for
he felt inadequate to express the beauty he imagined, the "elusive"
effect he aspired to achieve.

Neoplatonism

Hergesheimer first portrays a maudlin, earthly kind of beauty and
love found by Mrs. Stella Condon at various hotels from Lake George
to Florida. Just now she and her ten-year-old daughter are at the
Boscombe, presumably by the sea in Atlantic City. Mrs. Condon is
a warm, convivial blonde; and her daughter is a cool, blue-eyed
brunette. Linda, fiercely loyal to her pleasure-loving mother, is questioned by the ladies around the hotel because they think her parent
neglects her for private escapades with men. When the mother comes
home, sometimes drunk, she condemns men and warns Linda that
because love and marriage are separate, she should strike as good
a bargain in marriage as she can.

One night in the lounge Linda is addressed by a venerable stranger.
Howard Welles, who calls her Bellina, a name which together with
"Linda" identifies her with prettiness. Struck by her appearance, he
tells her she has a magical beauty which to stricken men "will be
more potent than any duty or fidelity."[6] Then he talks of the worship
of beauty in the Middle Ages, of magic, and of a lady riding on a
white mule or leopard. He mentions Plato, Cardinal Pietro Bembo,
Cosimo de Medici, and Pico della Mirandola, and he mystifies her
when he says, "The endless service of beauty. Of course, a woman—
but never the animal; the spirit always. Born in the spirit, served in
the spirit, ending in the spirit. A direct contradiction, you see, to
nature and common sense, frugality and the sacred symbol of the
dollar" (32-33). Shortly afterward, he quoted an Italian line,

> "*La figlia della sua mente, l'amorosa idea.*" (34)
> ("The daughter of the mind, the loving Idea.")

This unexpected conversation turns out to be a key to the novel.
Stella Condon continues her revels, but a clumsy beautician damages

her hair and, incidentally, forces an end to her convivial earthly love. She then marries the kindly Moses Feldt of New York. Through Judith, one of Mr. Feldt's daughters, Linda is invited to a party given by Markue, who entertained many persons interested in the art world. Linda chats with a young man, admires the statue of the Winged Victory, and meets Dodge Pleydon, a tall, powerful sculptor accompanied by Susanna Noda, his current feminine friend. Seeing the newcomer, he lifts Susanna from his lap and tells Linda, "You are Art— Art the deathless" (114). Linda takes the first step in her aesthetic education when she, feeling the power of the Winged Victory, comments on its lack of utility, and Dodge tells her art is "permanence given to beauty," something different from the plebeian conception of beauty as "oatmeal and scented soap" (115). Shortly thereafter her mother's advice returns to Linda's mind, and she reflects on marriage and the idea of losing herself in love. Susanna sees the coolness in Linda and calls it Siberia; and piqued at Dodge, she tells him that his work is not of first rank and he will become fat if he marries. He ignores her and takes Linda home, where her inner being protests when he kisses her.

Months later at an outdoor concert Linda meets Amelia Lowrie, a sister of her father. When she tells her mother, Stella informs her of how the husband had simply taken his hat one day and walked out, abandoning his enceinte wife. This chance meeting with Amelia leads to a visit to her father's old home in Philadelphia. She has refused marriage to Dodge, but she accepts the proposal of Arnaud Hallett, a nephew of the Lowrie sisters, and in time the couple have two children, named Lowrie and Vigné.

The remainder of the book concerns Dodge's growth from an inferior sculptor to a superior one and Linda's artistic education. As the years pass, Dodge produces work inspired by Linda: a statue of Cotton Mather, a bust of a charwoman in Philadelphia, and a statue of a visionary pioneer named Simon Downige in Hesperia, Ohio.

One day, like her father, Linda takes her hat and walks out, intending to live with Dodge; but when she arrives at his studio, he is absent. Soon he returns, and, not knowing her plan, he talks to her about her spirit and seeing her as a young girl at Markue's or even younger—ten. After Dodge shows her a faded glove he has saved for many years and explains that now her hand is less real than his dream of it, she becomes aware that he lives with his vision of her.

She returns to Philadelphia and realizes she has become middle-aged. Confirmation of that fact comes three years later when she over-hears her outspoken daughter-in-law telling Vigné that Linda has failed in appearance and that her skin has become dry. Then Linda realizes that Arnaud is failing, and a telegram announces Dodge's death.

After a period she determines to go to Cottarsport to see the one statue of Downige by Pleydon remaining after an ignorant mob had pulled down the one in Hesperia. Once on the site, Linda thinks of a lady riding a leopard, the Boscombe's marble columns and red carpet, Mr. Welles's speech, "the old gesture toward the stars" and the Italian line of poetry. And she thinks of Markue's party and of Dodge's statue of Simon Downige, who from his weary body gazed out with a vision of truth. Then, "She was choked by a sharp rush of joy at Dodge's accomplishment, an entire understanding of the beauty he had vainly explained, the deathless communication of old splendid courage, an unshaken divine need, to succeeding men and hope. This had been hers. She had always felt her presence in his success; but, until now, it had belonged exclusively to him. Dodge had, in his love, absorbed her, and that resulted in the statues the world applauded" (302). And now finally, "she could see that he had preserved her spirit, her secret self, from destruction. He had cheated death of her fineness. The delicate perfection of her youth would never perish, never be dulled by old age or corrupted in death" (302-3). She recalled Dodge's use of the word *katharsis* and felt she had entered the realm of eternal beauty through his later work.

Analysis and Estimate

In this period Hergesheimer's aestheticism was at its apogee: he recently had composed the brilliant surface beauty of *Java Head*, and in his review of Joseph Conrad's *Arrow of Gold* the quality he stressed was beauty. Now, when he sought to create an earthly picture of this quality, he turned to women as the natural embodi-ments of it, and for the first time he used a female protagonist. She serves not only as personified beauty but also as the inspiration for Dodge to rise from the earthly type to a vision of the universal kind. Hergesheimer's conception here follows his belief that "Practi-cally every created masterpiece in sound or words or stone or color was born of the response in a man's soul to the unutterable charm of a woman. To her charm, you see; not to her virtues as a housewife and faithful mother."[7] Hergesheimer implies that an artist is not inspired to the highest achievement by earthly attractiveness such as that of Stella Condon or Susanna Noda, for only when he is denied marriage to Linda does Pleydon gradually achieve his superior understanding of beauty.

The idea that Hergesheimer uses in this novel and that excited him so much is found in Plato's *Symposium*, in which Socrates explains it as he said he had heard it from Diotima of Mantinea. When the Renaissance began in Italy, the Platonic idea influenced Dante's *Vita Nuova*, Petrarch's sonnets, Marsilio Ficino and his Academy in Florence, Pico della Mirandola, and others. In Castiglione's *The Book of the Courtier* it is Pietro Bembo who expounds the conception now known as Neoplatonism. He describes the lack of satisfaction in sensual love, the need to love beauty in the abstract and, finally, to love beauty in its universal form. The result, he says, will be most fortunate: "Thus the soul, aflame with the most holy fire of true divine love, flies to unite herself with the angelic nature, and not only completely abandons sense, but has no further need of discourse of reason; so that transformed into an angel, she understands all things intelligible and beholds without veil or slightest cloud the wide sea of pure divine beauty and receives it into herself and enjoys that supreme happiness which cannot be grasped by the senses."[8] Bembo argues that only a mature man can arrive at this highest state because a young one will be entrapped by sensuality.

In *Linda Condon* the author follows this Neoplatonic conception quite closely. He shows Dodge at first as a womanizer whose sensuality will limit his achievement to second-rate work; but the sculptor, a mature man, is able to rise to loving beauty in its abstract and then in its universal form. The first sign of his purified work is the statue of Cotton Mather, which Arnaud recognized as having power. Then the bust of the charwoman at the Academy of Fine Arts follows; and when Linda is repelled by its coarseness, Dodge insists that it is beautiful, saying, "Pity, *Katharsis*—the wringing out of all dross." (p. 207). To make his point, he shows her a realistic ruffed grouse model which she thinks exceptionally well done; but he points out it is merely photographic. Next, the gazing blank eyes in the statue of Simon Downige are intended to suggest not only his dreams of

Hesperia but Dodge's vision of universal beauty, which was far beyond the mortal bodies of Cotton Mather, the charwoman, and Simon Downige.

Two points about Dodge's use of *katharsis* need clarification. First, Aristotle's conception of the purging of emotions through pity and fear was applied to mighty political figures while Hergesheimer applies it to fairly humble citizens. Cotton Mather, moreover, is difficult to understand in the company of a charwoman and a Utopian. Second, Dodge applied the word to sculpture rather than drama and limits it to pity. Whether Aristotle's emotional purgation would be caused by a different medium and by pity alone might be disputed.

Hergesheimer saw *Linda Condon* as partly autobiographical. Just as Linda lacked education, so did he; and when he ran across Neoplatonism, he found it explained what he had vaguely striven for in his attempts to serve "beauty" in his novels. Linda gradually understood Dodge's comprehension of universal beauty, and Hergesheimer in his maturity perceived it also. He presumably avoided the point of view of Dodge, the creative artist, so that he could maintain objectivity at the same time as he told the story of the pretty, blue-eyed young girl with dark hair and bangs.

The style is not noteworthy, though the passages describing Linda's insight into Dodge's vision as she sat at Cottarsport rise above the general level in the novel. The mannerisms, noted in preceding chapters, remain and, though not desirable, are not conspicuous. In the first portion of the book the description of decors appears too full, but there is the defense here that they fit the pattern of Platonism with the rise from the sensuous Boscombe and the Feldt home to the austere Lowrie house. These decors are the first in one of the author's contemporary novels.

Other aspects of his writing are handled with his customary ease. As Parrington perceived,[9] Hergesheimer seeks unity at the beginning partly through the symbolism of Linda's black bang: "A black bang was, but not ultimately, the most notable feature of her uncommon personality—straight and severe and dense across her clear pale brow and eyes" (9). He inconspicuously indicates the passage of time, expertly foreshadows coming action, and clearly distinguishes his characters. Linda, devoid of strong human emotions, seems less real than her mother. Hergesheimer created her cold, calling her an "icy little devil" after he had completed the novel.[10] At one time he thought of calling his essay in *Everybody's* "A Dedicatory Note for a Portrait in Alabaster," but he used the actual title instead.[11] In the novel itself Arnaud characterizes her as alabaster; and Hergesheimer presumably meant her to be exactly that. Perhaps the best of the minor characters are Stella Condon, depicted as maudlin in her revelry, and Moses Feldt, whose gentleness and generosity distinguish him from all the others.

The fact that Hergesheimer once again paints some minor characters more vividly than the major indicates a possible weakness in his art. The problem seems to stem more from lack of knowledge of people and consequent lack of interest in them than from any hostility toward humanity. His sickly youth, his home environment, the religious de-emphasis of the individual, and his lack of social success all contributed to his small knowledge of human character. Incidents such as the ones in hotels or in the art world, though, were part of his experience. When he wrote from this experience, he could produce clear-cut minor figures; but he had neither the knowledge nor the inclination to portray the characters in detail. He differentiates them by externals rather than by subtle traits. Thus Stella is blonde and Linda brunette, flowers wilt on Stella but remain fresh on Linda, Judith Feldt prefers Strauss but Linda prefers Gluck, and Dodge's kiss repels the young Linda but Arnaud's does not. There also is little character development in the ordinary sense. When Linda's refusal of marriage to Dodge causes him to rise to his potential of seeing the highest beauty, and when Linda herself gains an understanding of it, these changes are of comprehension rather than character.

In this book as well as in most of his others Hergesheimer deals with the well-to-do or wealthy. Fortunately for Linda, Arnaud was able to provide $50,000 dollars per year, though she had wanted twice that. Inasmuch as she is the incarnation of art (at least for Dodge), the reader wonders whether the author assumes that wealth is a necessary base for art.

A puzzling incident is Linda's leaving Arnaud for Dodge. The fact that the sculptor thinks she is merely visiting and tells her that his vision of her hand is more real than her hand itself reveals his Neoplatonic development, but the motivation for coming to him seems inadequate. When her father, distressed over such plebeian dishes as boiled cabbage, had picked up his hat one day and walked

out, he was disturbed by a cultural difference. But Linda was happy
with Arnaud, and her brief desertion of him seems less genuine,
serving only to reveal Dodge's Neoplatonic progress.

Linda Condon met with a mixed reception. After the successful
The Three Black Pennys and *Java Head* the new volume puzzled
readers and critics because they had expected another and even better
novel about the American past. The English critics generally gave
only moderate approval, despite Walpole's loyal support of his American friend (24 July 1920, 3 December 1919). Perhaps typical were
W. L. George, who thought the new novel less than the author's
peak, and Joseph Priestley, who maintained that Linda was unreal
as a person.[12] The novelist Priestley touched on a key problem of
whether Linda was deathless art and an extraordinarily beautiful
woman as well. As a woman, she seems to have the detachment of
universal beauty itself without enough traits to set her off as an
individual. Her appearance alone, without small characteristics and
habits or some emotional commitment, leaves her underdeveloped
as a human being. Priestley also sees the mental images in the first
pages as being excessive, a feature which could lead readers to think
of Hergesheimer as being only "decorative." In all these observations
Priestly is both discerning and accurate. Anonymous American critics
commended the psychology; the portrayal of Linda, Mrs. Condon, and
the Moses Feldt family; and the author's winning the reader's sym-
pathy for a self-centered devotee to her own beauty.[13] This last comment overstates the case because Linda wanted to lose herself in
love of her family but could not.

Two American critics writing for the British periodicals, *Athenaeum*
and *Spectator*, arrived at only qualified approval of the novel. In his
review of *Linda Condon* and of Cabell's *Jurgen*, Conrad Aiken, himself a writer, deplored the lack of good American fiction writers in
the last few years, maintaining that Hergesheimer and Cabell were
the only ones to gain prominence.[14] Aiken missed "the slow grave
beauty of style" found in *Java Head*, but he liked the portraits of
the women, calling them "vivid" and "charming," the best to date.
He thought the conception of Linda was exceptionally well done
and marveled at how she could grow but still keep her cool, childlike
composure. Aiken saw the novel as complementary to Henry James's
What Maisie Knew, though he imputed no indebtedness. The main
difference was that James's concern was solely with Maisie's childhood whereas Linda reaches middle age. A negative note is Aiken's

assessment that while he calls the book "delightful," he has no desire to reread it soon. Aiken's points are well taken. Most critics would not quarrel with any of them, but at the same time they would note his remark about rereading the book. This reaction is one that others have, probably because there is little emotional identification with the beauteous protagonist.

Van Doren, in 1920, stresses other points.[15] He included long quotations from Howard Welles in the Boscombe Hotel and Linda at Cottarsport as the author's best writing, and the paragraph on Judith and Pansy Feldt's friends as a sample of elaborate description. To him the book was about temperament, the name "Dodge Pleydon" was objectionable, and Linda was cold. These observations are sound; and his question of whether Hergesheimer was writing too much was apropos because at this time the author was composing short stories as well as novels. Building a novel on Neoplatonism was difficult enough without the pressure of time.

Hergesheimer's combining the ideas of a ten-year-old girl and Neoplatonism resulted in a qualified success. The author chose a subject that was difficult, especially for one who had neither education nor wide experience; but he wisely sought to convey Neoplatonism indirectly through its effect on the sculptor. He created a main female character different for him because Linda is beauty incarnate, while others from Ludowika onward tend to personify vigor more than sheer pulchritude. But despite Hergesheimer's initial enthusiasm for his subject, combining beauty in the concrete and in the abstract, he necessarily fell short of his goal; he wrote Cabell that the book was too esoteric for the general reader (22 December 1919); and he told Napier that the book failed because one cannot write about creative artists.[16] The subject is immensely difficult, and the hurried composition was not followed by careful rewriting. He sought to articulate a vision like Dodge's or Owen Warland's in Hawthorne's "The Artist of the Beautiful," so perfect and powerful that the destruction of a statue or a mechanical butterfly no longer mattered; but he lacked Hawthorne's control of his material. Hergesheimer did not succeed completely in reaching his Neoplatonic goal, but he made a remarkable attempt.

Chapter Six

Balisand and *The Limestone Tree*

On a slightly lower level than the preceding three novels are *Balisand* and *The Limestone Tree*, both rooted in the Americana the author loved. In the five years between *Linda Condon* and *Balisand* Hergesheimer published articles, travelogues, over thirty short stories, autobiography and three novels. All of them precede the leaner style that the author adopted in 1924 and kept for the remainder of his writing career.

Balisand

Published two years after *The Bright Shawl* and *Cytherea, Balisand* (1924) marks a return to a much earlier era in American life. Depicting the period from 1784 to 1800, years which saw the formation of the Constitution, the two terms of Washington as President and the one term of Adams, it treats Richard Bale and his adamant Federalism at a time when the social revolution accompanying the political and military one still continued. Quite appropriately, the setting is Tidewater Virginia, and, much of the time, specifically Balisand, a name derived from the inhabitants of a plantation—the Bales, now in the fourth generation from their Cavalier ancestor who migrated from England—and from sand showing in the river. Hergesheimer had thought of calling the story *Bale's Hundred*, but he chose rather *Balisand*, a name making possible the euphonious "Richard Bale of Balisand." Indicating Richard's nature is the epigraph on the flyleaf: *"the best tryall of a gentleman in bloud is by bearing of armes—Lord Coke."* He lived in the gentleman's world of gambling, drinking, fox hunting, politicking, horse racing, and parties. From seven years in the Revolutionary Army he had gained a fierce loyalty to Washington, a recurring pain in one leg, and disillusionment. From the Bales, Richard had acquired so much pride and courage and perhaps the contentiousness embodied in his uncle Morryson, who lived

54

with him, that, as the author wrote to Emma Gray, he was "as stiff . . . as starch."[1]

Like *Mountain Blood, Balisand* contains three parts separated by intervals of time; but unlike the earlier book, it has no chapters, only smaller units set off by three asterisks in the middle of the page. It is told largely through the consciousness of Richard Bale, the protagonist. Before he began writing, Hergesheimer took 150,000 words of notes;[2] and after composing the first two parts, he traveled to Virginia for additional specific facts for the third section. He wrote the story of 96,000 words in thirty-six days and dedicated it to his friend and publisher, Alfred A. Knopf.

Virginia story. As the novel opens, Richard Bale is being rowed by servants to the landing at Todd's Hundred, where Gawin Todd is giving a party to celebrate his engagement to Lavinia Roderick. The rowers sing an Anabaptist hymn as they cross the water on a hot day perfumed by the scents of roses, jasmine, and heliotrope. After landing, the bachelor Richard goes to his quarters above the schoolhouse, drinks steadily, and wonders whether he brought his hair-trigger pistols. He argues with a pious young schoolteacher, Mr. Garret, about love, drinks too much, misses dinner, and meets Ava (Mrs. Charles Todd), who encourages him to wed Mary, her oldest daughter; and the idea appeals to him. In the evening he wanders down to the little shelter at the end of the pier and soon becomes aware that a young lady is near him. It is Lavinia, for whom the party is being given. After they talk a bit, she sings,

> "A lilybud, a pink, a rose
> I send to you
> But you must bring me oceans more,
> Be true, be true."[3]

They converse for a time, and then she returns to the dancing; Richard thinks he doesn't like her, but she haunts his thoughts. He finds he is surrounded by romance—the tutor's yearning for Eliza Wiatt, the mocking birds, and Lavinia; and he offers the opinion to Eliza that love possibly is a poison.

The next day as Lavinia talks to him in the garden, the sunlight glances off her shoulder and, he thinks, temporarily blinds him. After a dinner accompanied by much imbibing and Federalist-Republican argument, Richard and Lavinia accidentally meet in the summerhouse.

They kiss, declare their love, and recognize the consequences. The shift in Lavinia's affections leads to the challenge of a duel between Gawin and Richard as the customary way for gentlemen to settle disputes. As preparations for the duel proceed, the partying goes on and Richard sends a yellow rose to Lavinia. In the evening as she is about to descend the stairs, she trips while singing "Be true—" and falls, strikes her head on the oaken floor, and dies. The duel is then called off.

The second part opens in 1793, nine years later. Horse racing, in which Richard wins; gambling, in which he loses; and politics dominate this section. In the political struggle between the Federalists and Democratic Republican forces Richard is staunchly the former. One day when he meets a man named James Luke on the road and discovers the French colors on his hat, he cuts Luke's face with a whip and has an English cockade sewn on his own hat. Then, in his strongest gesture of disdain for democracy, he acts as he considers a gentleman should when Luke brings a mob to Balisand. Richard goes up to Luke, shoots him in the head, turns away, and walks to the house without looking at the astonished crowd.

At the same time the romantic interest continues. Richard has recurring memories of Lavinia, especially when bright, flashing sunlight triggers them. Mary Todd has wed someone else, and Charles Todd has died. Ava, his widow, comes to Balisand one day and tells Richard that she now understands the problem between him and Gawin—she had discovered Lavinia's yellow rose in a box of gloves, but Gawin angrily destroyed it. Richard, though thinking that Gawin would pay in full for ruining the memento, told Ava that he himself had once said "love might be a poison" (164). At one time he is tempted to have an affair with Zena Gainge, the plebeian young wife of a retired sea captain, but he rejects the illicit love. Then as the second part ends, he proposes to the expert horsewoman Lucia Mathews, daughter of the wealthy Beverley Mathews. Though it has appeared that she has been about to marry Gawin Todd, she accepts Richard.

The events of the third part occur in 1800, seven years later. Lucia and Richard, who have three daughters, are happily married, but Richard at times still thinks of Lavinia. The political wars continue to keep Richard and Gawin antagonistic and finally lead to a dueling party, which meets before dawn. The two principals take their places; and when the men turn to fire, Richard is blinded by the rising sun.

As a result, he misses his shot but is bady wounded by Gawin's. Despite his weakness, he demands a second round. He is barely able to drag himself up against a tree; but when they fire again, he kills Gawin; and on the way home he dies just before the singing rowers get to the landing at Balisand. In his dying moments he thinks of Lavinia, returning in sunlight, as the cause of the argument with Gawin and ultimately of his own death. To him she now is "only a dead rose" (367).

Analysis and estimate.   Any estimate of the book's worth depends partly on Hergesheimer's intentions. He planned, first, to portray a region and an aristocratic breeding which he esteemed and understood. Percy Boynton, professor of English at the University of Chicago, sensed Hergesheimer's kinship with Richard Bale's world and said that the author "had a trait of highly developed formality coupled with an inherent independence of mind and conduct—the heritage of the non-conformist aristocrat. It belongs to all the black Pennys, Linda Hallet, Richard Bale, and Taou Yuen."[4] Hergesheimer admired Richard's pride and envied his courage, the quality which Hemingway would have called grace under pressure. At no time did the owner of Balisand betray his breeding, whether in gambling, horse racing, or dueling. Then, too, the author wished to give a picture of the early days of the Constitution and the birth of political parties. And he wanted to show Richard in a particular time and place as the product of heredity and environment, not as a person deciding his own fate in the Romantic sense.

How Hergesheimer came to choose his subject is not known, but he found the grace of the Southern and border states especially attractive. Earlier in life he had spent many months in the Virginia mountain country, had visited Cabell near Richmond, and had been guide, contributor, and friend to the *Reviewer*, Emily Clark's literary magazine in the Virginia capital. And the book gave Hergesheimer an opportunity to express his own attitude toward life. For him the Dower House was his Balisand.

As Hunter Stagg noted in the *Reviewer*,[5] the novel is as much a character study of Richard Bale as anything. At first it seems that romantic love will dominate the story, but it becomes apparent that Richard's inner and outer reactions to situations touching him closely are the subject. In gambling he is daring; in drinking, prodigious; in racing, skilled. And in all activities he is courageous. He is not afraid to duel or defy popular opinion whenever it goes against his code.

He is proud, wishing to have no catering to the general populace. He reflects once that in the new times *qui gerit arma* no longer refers only to gentlemen because the militia also carry guns. His dueling pistols are before us from the Todds' party to the conclusion.

When the author wrote to Emma Gray that he thought she would find a completely Virginian attitude in *Balisand*,[6] he obviously did not anticipate the irate reaction of the residents of that state who assumed that Hergesheimer intended to portray Richard Bale as typical of a Virginia gentleman. In his review of *Balisand*[7] Stagg stated the Virginians' objections to taking Richard as typical and listed points that would not fit the ordinary pattern for Virginia gentlemen. However, Stagg justified Richard's conduct by urging that he should be judged by the creed of his time that he was "divinely privileged" by birth and inheritance. Although Stagg praised the execution of the author's conception, he thought that the political issues would not be intelligible for those readers not already familiar with the period. In these strictures the reviewers raised valid points, for Richard let his bitterness dominate his gentlemanliness, and the politics are too complex to explain easily.

A balanced appraisal of the new novel was published in the *New York Times*: "From the first page to the last the reader is impressed by the care he has taken with details, the cold lapidary researches that must have gone into the elaboration of his atmosphere. . . . Only when it comes to the action of the story is one disappointed, for there is no action. The story is essentially the study of a single character. It is a study in intransigeance rather than action, pathos rather than tragedy, the character which alters not while all else changes. As such it is ironical and the end is suavely satirical. . . ."[8] The anonymous reviewer is accurate in his citing of care in details, lack of plot, and Richard's intransigence; and he may be correct in calling the ending "suavely satirical." In the available correspondence, though, there is no hint that the author intended satire in the sentimental ending. Several of the periodical reviews were primarily negative, but enough were positive that Hergesheimer wrote to Knopf about what he thought were his first favorable reviews in five years (9 October 1924).

Perhaps the greatest problem concerns the nature of Richard. In a letter to [Laurence] Stallings of the *New York World* Hergesheimer said, "I am, I suppose, a Federalist in temperament . . . and so a great deal of Richard Bale's feeling was natural to me—natural and at the same time largely made articulate by the best feeling of the best boys

intimately known to me who were actually in the late war. A cousin
specially, very close to me indeed, brought back a fine dark satirical
bitterness, an incurable remoteness from the daily important, to which,
in Balisand [*sic*] I was enormously indebted" (30 September 1924).
To the author's Federalist temperament and to the post-World War I
"satirical bitterness" of American soldiers should be added his liking
for self-assertive heroes. But difficulties arise. If Richard usually was
determined by outside influences, why did he often seem less sociable
than his peers, including other veterans? As it is, he appears agreeable only when compared with his uncle, Morryson. Richard has his
virtues as a Virginia gentleman, but they are less perceptible than
his frequent testiness. It is likely that Richard seems less objectionable to the author than to the general reader.

As usual in Hergesheimer, the characters are distinct and often
opposites. Among the men, the Richard-Garret and Richard-Gawin
contrasts are the most prominent; and among the women, the Lavinia-
Zena, Zena-Lucia, and Lucia-Lavinia are outstanding. Lavinia is decorative and impractical, Zena is attractive but common, and Lucia
is pretty, proficient with horses, and competent with children. Lavinia,
in the pattern of Ludowika, attracts him with her vigor: "She was
very handsome, principally because of the brilliant temper of her
youth. The emotion he had got from her voice alone, that sharp
vitality, was infinitely increased by her whole presence" (50). Richard
falls in love with Lavinia, who may represent inspirational love; he
flirts briefly with Zena, who is merely physical love; and he loves
Lucia, who is the personification of genuine affection. And Ava is the
efficient, compassionate mother figure comparable to Rhoda in *Java
Head*.

Partly because of persistent charges of descriptive ornateness, Hergesheimer ignored the advice of his friend Walpole (2 April 1923)
and adopted a sparer style beginning with *Balisand*. Oddly enough,
several critics praised him for descriptive passages despite their rarity;
and Hergesheimer complained to Cabell that no one had seemed to
notice how he had simplified his writing (27 September 1926).
Here he was mistaken because Stagg complained of a lack of period
atmosphere[9] and Van Doren also noted the change,[10] which produced
passages such as the following:

It was still dark when, the following morning, Little York woke him;
but when he was shaved and had dressed, the sky beyond the North

River was bright with dawn. There was, yet, no breakfast, and he had a hard biscuit and a glass of brandy. On the left of the plantation, partly through what was called the river field and part beyond, there was an oval track with an exceeding modest stand, some board seats laid across supports with a covering; the woods between that and the public way were so thick, so treacherous with marsh, as to be impassable; and there Richard Bale worked and ran his horses. (170)

That Hergesheimer intended a major change is apparent in his statement to Stallings that he "deliberately threw all furnishings overboard —the beautiful early black walnut, the rosy muslins and panniered brocades, the powdering rooms and deep ruffles" (30 September 1924). One result of his change was a shift from visual appeal to that of other senses, especially hearing and smell.

The period chosen by Hergesheimer saw the rise of political parties and the struggle over British and French influences. In depicting the period the author has taken on an extremely difficult task. To master the intricacies of the political currents of the time is a venture for years rather than months, so that the material can be thoroughly digested. At times, as in the second part, the political development seems obtrusive rather than functional.

Several points contribute to making *Balisand* readable. There is a roundedness to the novel which is satisfying: Richard opens the story crossing the water in a canoe rowed by hymn-singing servants, and he returns at the end, dying, in the same way. The changing times are clearly indicated by alterations in dances, clothes, drinks, and politics. The three parts of the novel lend balance. Unity is strengthened by leitmotifs such as Lavinia's song, glancing sunlight, the yellow rose, the Federalism, and the testy Bale temper, exemplified in its excess by the uncle, Morryson Bale. Furthermore, readers familiar with the *Aeneid* will recognize that the name Lavinia has some appropriateness because in the Latin epic Lavinia would have married Turnus had not Aeneas come across the water; and the quarrel over her ended in a duel between the two champions, resulting in the death of Turnus.

In a perceptive article analyzing Hergesheimer's novels Joseph Priestley observed that many have the quality of a dream.[11] In some respects this insight applies to *Balisand*, but there should be the qualification that it be a daydream. In it the author can make all parts fit together, and in *Balisand* the parts do fit with unusual exactitude. In Lavinia's song, for instance, the first line ends with a rose, and Richard sends a rose; the last line adjures the listener to "be true," Lavinia sings those as her last words, and for nine years Richard remains true to her memory. The foreshadowing is careful and exact because in the daydream all parts can be imagined to fall into place better than in actuality.

In *Balisand* Hergesheimer returned to the Neoplatonism he had incorporated into *Linda Condon* and *The Lay Anthony*. In the former he had written of reaching the conception of pure beauty, as Pleydon did with his statue of Simon Downige. In *The Lay Anthony* the Neoplatonism is that of Dante, Petrarch, and Boccaccio in their poetic tributes to the deceased Beatrice, Laura, and Filomena. In *Balisand* it is the dead Lavinia who is remembered; but there is a startling difference: rather than an inspiration, she becomes a memory to be exorcised, a torment for Richard from which he is freed only by a fatal wound.

Balisand possesses many merits as a portrayal of the times, the characters, and the region. Individual portions, such as the opening and closing chapters and horse racing, are particularly well done. Unfortunately, the reader does not understand how the protagonist can possess so many strengths but be so unlikable. More deliberate writing might have resulted in a more understandable or acceptable figure, but Hergesheimer seemed to take pride in his rapid composition.

The Limestone Tree

After *Balisand* came *From an Old House, Tampico, Quiet Cities, Swords and Roses*, and *The Party Dress*; then in *The Limestone Tree* (1931), his last successful novel, Hergesheimer returned to the past, the source of most of his best books. This time he set his story inland in Kentucky, a state whose people fit his preference for masculine men and ladies esteemed especially for "beauty and feeling."[12] He thought the state ideal with its strong geographical and cultural contrasts, a place "unlike Virginia, totally and always American."[13] He sought to capture the spirit of Kentucky through the intertwined generations of the Sashes, the Abels, and the Hazels. Their nature can be gathered from what Gabriel once said to his daughter, Camilla: "You are, I will repeat it, a Sash. A violent and passionate and faithful family.

I am always afraid of it; I am afraid of myself; I am afraid of you."[14]
The families were not prominent people but their natures are indicated by the name of the protagonist in the last chapter—Folkes.

The idea for the volume seems to have grown out of Hergesheimer's
association with the *Post*'s George Lorimer. As early as May 1927
the two were planning a trip to Kentucky; and after the trip, he
wrote to Lorimer about plans for a three-part paper on their Kentucky
visit, but he changed his mind and a little over a year later informed
Lorimer that he had begun background work on the novel suggested
by his correspondent. Then he wrote the editor that he was still pre-
paring for the book on Kentucky, and on the same day (27 December 1928) he wrote Cabell about his plan to deal with a single
family over many years in a story with a ten-part structure, like the
belletristic *Quiet Cities.*

In September 1929 he sent Lorimer the first part of *The Limestone
Tree* with a note stating that instead of using an introduction he
had worked "the background and spirit of" the novel into the first
section.[15] When he had completed the third part two months later,
he was pleased enough with the work to that date to write Cabell
enthusiastically. The next July, when the serial publication was completed, he wrote Knopf that the volume was the only one of his to
be entirely rewritten after supposedly being in final form and that
it expressed his intentions better than any of his other books (26
July 1930). It was published first in the *Saturday Evening Post* (23
November 1929 to 12 July 1930) and then in Knopf's fine edition
(2 January 1931).

Kentucky story.   Deriving its title from the famous limestone
and bluegrass area of Kentucky, *The Limestone Tree* covers the extended period from 1775 to 1890, second in time span only to *The
Three Black Pennys.* Beginning with the hunter, successive generations of Sashes, Abels, and Hazels are settlers, soldiers, lawyers, and
farmers in "the most fatal land on the circumference of the globe"
(5). One hundred and fifteen years after the novel opens John Dixon
Folkes, born and reared in France, concludes it by visiting Kentucky
and deciding to live there.

The tone of the book is set in the first chapter, which tells of the
dangers and human cost involved in winning the state for the white
man. After the hunters and the bloody military expeditions of exploration, the pioneers come, often having to live in forts. Among the early
settlers is the family of James Abel, which is united with the hunting

stage of civilization by the marriage of Nancy Abel to Gabriel Sash, one of an early group called the "Long Hunters" because they had stayed in the Kentucky area for many months before they returned to Virginia. Gabriel and Nancy have a son, James, but the lure of the woods pulls the hunter away from his family, and he disappears into the primeval forest, never to be heard from again. Nancy, "like hickory," is strong enough to raise her boy in the dangerous and beautiful world of early Kentucky. Thus in the first chapter are established the attractiveness and richness of the "fatal land" as a setting and the nature of the white immigrants, people courageous, tenacious, dependable, and honorable.

The next two chapters add details about the ruggedness of the pioneers. In the first of the two the theme of danger from the South is established through the story of Nancy Sash. When her Uncle John returns from New Orleans with both pro-Spanish sentiments and a Spanish wife, trouble is almost certain. Because Nancy thinks John's wife Laure is casting a spell on James, she kills Laure, but she escapes punishment when her father and Beriah Mace warn John to be silent. In the following chapter James Sash has become an adult, has married, and has lost through death the mother of his young daughter, Nancy. After fighting in the War of 1812 James returns to his successful law practice. Seeing the novice nun Linda Rozier and falling in love with her, he shortly persuades her to run away with him and marry.

The fourth story tells of political assassination and revenge, and succeeding chapters include horse racing, a widow's attempt to keep her son out of the Civil War, rivalry in love, voluntary spinsterhood, and finally the decision by the French John Dixon Folkes to remain in Kentucky. Coincident with his decision comes the death of the second Gabriel Sash, which, together with the repetition of evocative passages from preceding chapters, creates a sense of unity and completeness in the book.

Analysis and estimate.   When Hergesheimer had finished *The Three Black Pennys*, he insisted it was not a historical novel. Only by a very loose definition of the term could it or *The Limestone Tree* have been said to be one, although they appear to overlap with the categories listed by Royal A. Gettmann in a *Dictionary of World Literary Terms.*[16] Hergesheimer had exactitude of research for detail, for example; but he was very selective in the details he chose as confirmed in a letter to Adelaide Neal, *Saturday Evening Post* editor, in which he said, "I am engaged in the business of emotions and not facts; and, although the facts must be correct, there is a necessary choice among them" (1 August 1922). As Sara Haardt pointed out, by writing, Hergesheimer escaped into an imaginary world as he had in youthful years;[17] and in this world, he used the past to get the aesthetic effects he wanted, but there was no intention of writing history as such. Ronald E. Martin supports this view when he says, ". . . Hergesheimer did not depict history, he used it."[18] The author made *The Limestone Tree* an aesthetic escape to the American past in which the wanderlust of the hunters, the travails of the pioneers, the sacrifices of the succeeding generations, and the bitter family divisions of the Civil War revealed how heroic mankind could be. To achieve his effect, he ran a thread of pride, courage, and honor through the society that evolved in the land of limestone and bluegrass.

For *The Limestone Tree* Hergesheimer made some changes both in structure and style. By the time he composed it, he had become dissatisfied with the novel as a form because he felt it difficult to express his intentions and his attitude toward life; and he also had become weary of following a protagonist's career for a full book. Coming in his adulthood to look at human life as meaningless but glorified by courageous individual acts, he preferred a panoramic view involving many persons over many decades, in this instance in ten stories.

He maintained the less ornate style of *Balisand*, even being colloquial when reporting a character's recollections, as when James Abel ponders: "Yes, it was all very confusing, the state of his own affairs and the doings in the world. He continued, for the moment, to study on the wider aspects of existence—the newly adopted Federal Constitution for example. Kentucky had voted agin it and he wasn't sure but that she was wrong. What, after all, had they fit England for?" (41) Even more colloquial is the remembrance of the sixteen-year-old Nancy Abel: "A very nice boy, John Skelp, who had kissed her, afterwards told Nancy to her face that he would as lieve [*sic*] kiss a scalping knife. In return Nancy had been fierce. Who had ast him to try it, she demanded. She didn't want him akissing her. It was just a happen so he hadn't ketched a slap across his jaw" (16). Such colloquial language, adopted by Hergesheimer for the first time, defined the nature of the person and his social level. The *Times Literary Supplement* reviewer praised the writing: "The prose, half colloquial, half formal, is woven in a pattern at once deliberate and delicate; it grows simpler and lovelier, more characteristic but less mannered—and more effective."[19] About the prose some would differ. Fanny Butcher of the *Chicago Tribune* preferred the author's earlier style, but others made no lament over the change.[20]

The story involving the clash between Manoah's sense of honor and Nancy's "fixed allegiance to certain inner principles and necessities" (125) is one of the best in the book. Told with an admirable restraint, it has many small touches that heighten the pathos. For example, when Manoah comes to tell of the assassination of James, the children are playing and a nurse softly laughs; and Manoah stands silent with clenched fists until James's wife screams with her recognition that her husband has died. Later, as Manoah and Nancy sit striving to adjust to the tragedy, the footsteps of the children and nurses in the passageway are audible. Then when Nancy is still affectionately striving to keep Manoah from taking revenge, their words are exchanged in the quiet of dusk. After he finally chooses "obligations greater than any individual necessity" (135), his decision is marked by the unpleasant scraping of the chair as he rises to seek out Bensalem for killing. Following the deed, he violently wipes his dry hands on a handkerchief.

Chapter 5 reveals a different aspect of the best Kentucky character. When Fauche Brimage conspires to win bets by throwing a horse race, the second Gabriel Sash regards paying those bets as a matter of honor, though he has not made them. For years Gabriel and his wife had wanted a farm of their own, but he decided that he had to pay $10,000 to Thomas Hazel and $5,000 to the widow of Jarrot Bensalem, the man who had assassinated his father. Thus did he exemplify a sense of honor which Hergesheimer took to be one of the nobler Kentucky traits.

According to Napier, in this novel "There is a final reconciliation of the opposite poles of temperament and heritage he expressed in *The Lay Anthony* and *Mountain Blood*."[21] The temperament was that of an aesthete, and the heritage was the morality of Woodnest. Since the days of his apprentice novels Hergesheimer had matured in both categories. In setting his story in the region of limestone, bluegrass, buckeyes, blue ash, and honey locusts; in the effect of each story; and in the emotional power of the Civil War in American life, he created a powerful aesthetic impact. By depicting character in the actions of Nancy Sash, James Sash, Manoah Abel, and the second Gabriel Sash, Hergesheimer brought together the aesthetic and the moral just before his 1930 illness damaged his creative powers.

Although the book received some negative comment, it was favorably reviewed by most critics. Writing in the *Bookman*, the respected critic Louis Kronenberger found many faults in *The Limestone Tree*.[22] For him, the author was dated, attempting to make the bluegrass region glamorous and portraying insignificant, wasted lives of persons who did not confront life. Here, it seems, Kronenberger is a bit snobbish, and ironically attacks Hergesheimer for faithfully writing about the "common man" after the years the novelist had been criticized for concerning himself with only the rich. Kronenberger's point that the characters do not "come to grips with life" is true enough, but the author was more interested in the panorama of picturesque or intense moments rather than in the individual. Kronenberger also thought the idea of John Dixon Folkes's settling in Kentucky "absurd," the story "pretentious," and the author mistaken in thinking the glamorous is significant. The critic apparently did not realize what Hergesheimer was trying to do—to create an aesthetically pleasurable volume rather than a meaningful one.

The anonymous reviewer in the *Times Literary Supplement*, taking a positive view, caught the author's philosophy underlying the novel:

The book is—what distinguishes it at once from the ordinary "romantic" recreation of the past—informed with the pitilessness, the irrevocability, of life; but set against that, what gives it its power of appeal, its "bitter beauty," is that sense of a personal integrity which alone can offset "the evasions and lies that make up the treachery of living." That is "the obligation of honour" to which Mr. Hergesheimer, revealing a kinship with Conrad deeper than any surface influence, constantly returns, an individual obligation which is yet "greater than individual necessity, more than any man's hopes of happiness."[23]

Here the reviewer correctly senses Hergesheimer's attitude toward life as it existed since the time of *From an Old House*. Hergesheimer did not look forward to a future life, but he insisted on a present one with honor. Despite the critical success of *The Limestone Tree*, it did not sell well. The Great Depression, still worsening, inevitably contributed to the changed taste dominating the Thirties, which resulted in Hergesheimer's loss of popularity. Knopf recognized the worth of the volume, though, and at one time thought of reissuing it.[24]

These two novels, though not quite up to the standard of *The Three Black Pennys* and *Java Head*, are the author's last successes about early days. They mark a departure from business subjects and move southward to the states of Virginia and Kentucky from the settings in Massachusetts and Pennsylvania. Both *Balisand* and *The Limestone Tree* emphasize patriotism: in the former, Richard's loyalty is to George Washington and to the United States for which they both fought; and in the latter the issue of loyalty to the Federal government is prominent. Structurally the two novels are quite different, but stylistically they are the same, except for the dialect in *The Limestone Tree*. Both use far less description and omit pictures of decor. Hergesheimer did not specify his reasons for his change, but it may be that he was reacting to those critics who steadily censured his earlier penchant for lavish description. Whatever the reason, the altered style provides greater emphasis on the inner "necessities" of the main characters. Perhaps more important is a difference in polish between the two books. As Hergesheimer's only novel rewritten completely after being in supposedly final form, *The Limestone Tree* has a finish his other novels do not possess. *Balisand* needed such rewriting. Had it been rewritten, Richard might have become a more congenial character than the one who incomprehensibly to the reader was the favorite of almost all the ladies, despite his excessive drinking and generally irascible attitude toward the world.

Chapter Seven

Minor Novels

In addition to the preceding novels, Hergesheimer penned seven others of lesser value. "Steel" (1920) and "Demeter, A Farm Woman" (1936), the first and last of these, were published only in the *Saturday Evening Post*. Of those remaining, four can be analyzed in pairings: *The Bright Shawl* (1922) and *Tampico* (1926) as the author's Latin-American novels, and *Cytherea* (1922) and *The Party Dress* (1930) as his comments on contemporary folly in middle-aged disciples of Venus. *The Foolscap Rose* (1934), the other novel, is a multi-generational account of a paper manufacturing family.

The Bright Shawl

The Bright Shawl is a tale of youthful patriotic idealism in Cuba at a time when she was waging a fight for independence. From his youth, the author could remember the flurry of excitement that engulfed the United States at the time of the Spanish-American War; and he had visited Cuba more than once, stayed in Havana and Camaguey, and learned firsthand something of local customs such as bull fighting, cock fighting, and *brujeria* ("black magic"). Many facets of *The Bright Shawl* were clearly outlined two years earlier in *San Cristóbal de la Habana* in which he tells of seeing a *mantón* in a Havana shop window, of watching Doloretes dance in New York, and of constructing a tale that would bring out the color, passion, and oppression of Havana. Dedicated to the author's friends Phoebe and Hamilton Gilkyson, Jr., the 30,000-word *The Bright Shawl* was published in *Redbook* (June–September 1922) and then as a book on 6 October.

Liberty.   The story is framed by contemporary scenes of the elderly Charles Abbott's disappointment over the lack of idealism in soldiers returning from World War I. When a neighbor plays

Liszt's "Spanish Rhapsody," its *jota* measure makes his mind drift back to when he was twenty-three and willing to sacrifice himself for Cuban independence. At that age, Charles embarked for Cuba because of weak lungs; and on ship he met Domingo Escobar, who was returning to his family in Havana. This chance meeting led to revolutionary activity with the son Andrés Escobar and three friends, all of whom favored independence from Spain.

The young men admired La Clavel, a striking Andalusian dancer with a bright *mantón*. Somewhat surprisingly, she took a fancy to Charles; and at the same time she discouraged the Spanish officer Santacilla, who watched the young men for subversive signs. Charles pretended to be in love with La Clavel, but he was so stricken with the patriotic Cuban ideal that he rejected her as well as Narcisa, the young sister of Andrés. After La Clavel killed Santacilla, the events headed toward a sad conclusion. A female spy from Peru killed Andrés, and Charles was deported.

As an old man he remembers his futile but glorious goal. The people next door return and waken him from his revery; and, confused, he rises "with outstretched arms as though he were grasping vainly for the dissolving fragments of a shining mirage of youth."[1] On the neighbor's piano someone plays a bit more of "The Spanish Rhapsody," and Charles goes to the table and his cold supper. From the cupboard he takes a bottle of Marquis de Riscal and drinks toasts, particularly to La Clavel and Andrés, dear friends from the days of shining idealism.

Analysis and estimate. *The Bright Shawl* is the most purely aesthetic of Hergesheimer's novels. As such, it would not gain everyone's approval, for not all critics either understood or appreciated the author's intention. Perhaps the most thorough and perceptive review was that by Joseph Wood Krutch, who in the *Nation* called it "perfect of its kind," noted little character drawing or psychology, and maintained that "Any unfavorable criticism that might be made would have to be directed against [the author's] aims."[2]

This charming minor novel deserves the critical accolades it received in its day. It captures the author's regretful opinion that the old American idealistic spirit was vanishing, a spirit so strong that Charles insists upon fraternal affection rather than love. The style is substantially the same as in the preceding novels, but, as Mencken pointed out, there is the tautologous "the El Louvre."[3] Unfortunately the style is the literary equivalent of impressionistic painting and is too open to easy parody. When, for example, the author identifies La Clavel's feelings with the shawl's colors, he writes that "the scarlet and magenta and burning orange and blue were her visible moods, her capriciousness and contempt and variability and searing passion" (55). One parodist wrote of "the Shawl—that orange, blue, emerald, scarlet, magenta, vermilion, crimson atrocity."[4] Though the style can thus be made to produce bathos, it served Hergesheimer well in creating a vivid impression of danger, cruelty, and insidious spying in pre-revolutionary Cuba.

Many other points about this short novel contribute to the unified aesthetic effect. In the name *La Clavel*, for instance, the author may have been suggesting the forceful stamping of the dance and a flower. The latter might be a pink, or it might be the common marigold— *clavel de muerto*, with the connotation of death. There are ironies, such as Charles's rejection of the love of Narcisa and La Clavel, the scenes of Venus in the fencing room, and Andrés's foolish affection for the murderous Pilar. There is coincidence, such as the sound of roosters crowing immediately after Santacilla figuratively has crowed over Charles. There are appropriate symbols, too. When the would-be assassin shoots the reflection in the mirror rather than the man he is stalking, he presages the entire revolutionary failure. And the best of the symbols is the *mantón* itself. On La Clavel it represents freedom, but on Pilar, treachery. For Charles it is a symbol of his life:

The shawl was a map, a representation, of the country of the spirit through which he passed; such emotions, such heat, and such golden roses, all had been, were, his against that background of perilous endeavor. It seemed to float up from the bed and to reach from coast to coast, from end to end, of Cuba; its flowers took root and grew, casting about splendor and perfume; the blue widened into the sky, the tenderness of the clasping sea; the dark greens were the shadows of the great ceiba trees, the gloom of the jungles, the massed royal palms of the plains. (168)

The book is the last of the kind readers had come to expect from Hergesheimer. It is a salute to the confident aestheticism that had dominated his novels from 1917 to 1922, the years of his greatest popularity. Later it was made into a movie starring Dorothy Gish and Richard Barthelmess.

Tampico

The idea for *Tampico* seems to have been suggested to Hergesheimer early in 1925 when he visited Mexico as a guest of its government.[5] Atypically a story of action, this novel tells of the Mexican oil fields in the days before nationalization, when the earlier roughshod behavior of the American companies gives way to corporate efficiency and deceit. The center of consciousness is Govett Bradier, a formerly dynamic field boss whose great achievement is the sea terminal which he built at Chorreras. He has become reflective during his eighteen months away from Mexico and gradually comes to reevaluate his life's purposes. To tell his story, the author divided his book into three parts: "The Sea Terminal," "Zacamixtle," and "La Calentura"; and he used no chapters, only small breaks marked by three asterisks. Published first in *Harper's Bazaar* (March 1926–August 1926), it appeared shortly after as a book (17 September 1926). Later Bartlett Cormack adopted it for the stage.

Mexican oil. In "The Sea Terminal" we meet the forty-year-old Bradier as his ship comes into Tampico harbor. He is returning from company headquarters in New York for unknown reasons; and, though he formerly was a high official, no one is sure of his present position in the Alianza Petroleum Corporation. He debarks, goes to a hotel, and then visits one of the cafés he had frequented before malaria forced him to leave a year and a half earlier. Gradually the reader senses that Bradier is entering danger.

As the story unfolds, Bradier visits G. K. Lentz, the Alianza office manager in Tampico and the sea terminal at Chorreras, now in the charge of Presby Corew. Shortly after he arrives, the reason for his return is learned: Vida, the wife of Presby. About twenty-seven, she is tan, slender, and romantic; but her short hair and her resemblance to a head on a coin suggest a certain masculine hardness. In a moment of reflection Bradier asks himself what of permanent value the hard-won oil will make possible. As the first part ends, Bradier undergoes a malaria attack.

The next section opens with his climbing the tower in the marine building for a look around the territory. He plans to leave soon, and Vida will follow; but in the meantime he wants to discover who lies behind the attacks on the terminal. He goes out into the field and then visits General Rayon, leader of the Mexican bandits. After returning, he thinks of his romance and realizes that Vida really wants sensation rather than him or any other man specifically. He admires her for her vitality, and he has come to like Presby for his resurgent courage. He finds Vida is impatient because of postponement of the trip north and she begins acting cool.

The third division commences with the early history of the Vida-Bradier affair and his present awareness that he can live without her. Bradier thinks he has enough evidence that Lentz is behind the Alianza troubles and Presby's assassination, but his efforts to prove guilt are thwarted by Vida's perfidy and his recurrence of malaria. Despite his being right, he is forced to leave Mexico surreptitiously. Resting on deck and looking at the sky as the ship moves out into the Gulf, Bradier concludes that none of the stars is ultimately important and the entire phenomenal universe will disappear as does a note on the ship's bell—in an "immensity of silence."

Analysis and estimate.   Although *Tampico* was not well received by the critics at the time, Martin has said that it "deserves more attention than it has received. It is probably Hergesheimer's most thoroughgoing, vivid attempt to depict the man involved in both business and romance."[6] This estimate more accurately evaluates the novel. Some critics objected to the portrayal of Vida, but she is no more sensation-hungry than Hemingway's Brett nor harder than his Mrs. Macomber. The psychology of Bradier from beginning to end rings true, but the gloating of Lentz in the hospital is melodramatic and should have been omitted. The equal subdivisions seem artificially composed of the same length. The author successfully evokes a feeling of danger as in "Wild Oranges," and vividly contrasts the bygone days of oil-field exploration with the newer times of corporate management, which are just as brutal but more sophisticated. Once again the author reveals admiration for courage and strength, though their possessor may be defeated, as was Bradier. The arrival on a ship at the opening and departure on one at the end suggest human arrival from infinity and departure into it. A new note is sounded in *Tampico*, however: when the protagonist loses because of malaria and Vida's perfidy, Hergesheimer goes beyond his philosophy that individuals are unimportant to the nihilistic view that mankind and the entire phenomenal universe are unimportant as well. All in all, the story, as Martin estimates, seems worthy of considerable praise.

There are significant differences in tone, structure, and style between *The Bright Shawl* and *Tampico*. The former is somber and reflective at the beginning and end but occasionally buoyant in the Cuban portion. The latter novel has a tone more world-weary than Ecclesiastes, implying, in effect, that the universe and all in it may be purposeless accidents. In *The Bright Shawl* the story is framed by the contemporary scenes about Charles Abbott at the beginning and end, but in *Tampico* the same effect is achieved by the arrival on a ship and the departure on one. The styles differ somewhat: *The Bright Shawl* is dominated by visual richness, while the other is in the more factual manner adopted in *Balisand*. Typical are two passages: "The room was long, tiled, and had, against the far wall, a great mirror which held in reverse the gay sweep of the tables, the heavily powdered shoulders of women, the prismatic flashes of diamonds and men's animated faces. The reflections were almost as fascinating as the reality, and Charles gazed from one to the other" (*The Bright Shawl,* 43). Contrasting is a passage from *Tampico*: "The room was long and narrow; at one end there was a railed gallery, hung with Spanish moss, and the other was occupied by the limited orchestra. The floor was crowded with dancers, the tables correspondingly empty, and Govett Bradier and Deas waited until they could find an unoccupied place."[7] The move away from aestheticism can be seen also in the diction which rarely found favor with the newspaper critics.

Among similarities between these two novels about Latin America are use of the modern era, the friendship of two men in times of great emotional stress, and a feeling of threatening evil. Again they incorporate Hergesheimer's favorite idea of courage in the face of impossible odds which defeat the protagonist. Just as the author regarded Richard Bale as happy in death because he had maintained his principles, so the reader can see Charles Abbott and Govett Bradier as triumphant despite apparent defeat. They, too, acted with honor and courage.

In two novels treating the collision between illicit middle-aged love and social conventions the conflict is described from the point of view of the man in *Cytherea* (1922) and from that of the woman in *The Party Dress* (1930). The author himself acknowledges the unusual direct pairing in a letter to Leon Kelley when he wrote about *The Party Dress*, "Naturally it is *Cytherea* reconsidered by a woman" (20 September 1930). Both books reflect the postwar upset in morals and conventions, telling of the loss of ideals, the restlessness, the frantic pursuit of sensation, the iconoclasm, and the impulse toward self-destruction so prominent in the 1920s.

Cytherea

In *Cytherea* Hergesheimer narrates Lee Randon's struggle at age forty-seven between an impulse toward an undefined fulfillment and society's mores. We have no record of how Hergesheimer happened to develop the story, though we do know that Mencken often urged him to apply his novelistic gifts to contemporary society and that five years earlier in *The Three Black Pennys* the author referred to "the fixed, painted impudence of a cynically debased doll" (154–55). He made that toy the main symbol of *Cytherea* and drew on the ample material in the rapid changes of postwar times, some of it at the golf club just across the road from the Dower House, where the author himself played.

At one time Hergesheimer considered calling the novel "Cythera," the name of the island where Aphrodite landed; then he changed the title to "Cytherea" to indicate a goddess of dominating, compulsive love. When the story was finished, he tried to sell it to Lorimer, but he was unsuccessful, probably because in 1922 it was not suited to the *Post* readership. The book appeared in a limited edition at Christmas, 1921, and in the trade edition on 3 January 1922. Because it was regarded as daring, bookstores often did not display it; yet it became the most popular of Hergesheimer's novels, selling 38,000 copies in less than three months and being made into a movie.

Love goddess.   Hergesheimer opens the tale in Eastlake (West Chester?) with Lee Randon golfing alone on a chilly November day. Apparently wealthy, successful in business, and happy in his marriage to Fanny, Lee actually feels restless; and shortly his independence, vague artistic impulses, and dissatisfaction with convention become prominent. In New York he has bought a doll with an enigmatic expression. Feeling its promise of enticing wickedness, he engages in silly golf club flirtations and sits on the stairs to talk with women at the home parties. Meanwhile, he believes that life with Fanny is reducing him to the human equivalent of the pig in the backyard pen; marriage has come to seem like flypaper.

In developing his story, Hergesheimer sends Lee on a mission to break up a romance which Peyton Morris, husband of Lee's niece Claire, is having with the movie actress Mina Raff (based partly on Lillian Gish). Lee is successful in breaking up Peyton's affair, but he becomes involved in one of his own with the passionate Savina Grove, who for him is the doll Cytherea come to life. When Lee's wife, Fanny, becomes suspicious, he is angry and takes Savina to Cuba, where, after a brief stay in Havana, the pair take a train to Camaguey, near which Lee's brother Daniel runs a plantation. Because of visitors already at the *estancia*, Lee and Savina are forced to stay in town in a vivid blue hotel room which she hates. Almost immediately she develops a fever and dies, and the doctor summoned from Camaguey diagnoses the killer as "excesses." Some weeks later Lee and Daniel sit talking one evening at the *estancia*, and the latter offers some wisdom to Lee: "This conventionality, that you have been so severe with, is exceedingly useful. It's not too much to say indispensable. Under its cover a certain limited freedom is occasionally possible."[8] Lee replies at length about the biological drive and the problem of having the truth make one free. He thinks he and Savina have acted according to the truth, but he does not know what it is for which the truth freed them. He receives one sort of answer in his discovery that Daniel has fallen asleep.

Analysis and estimate. In *Cytherea* Hergesheimer records some of the confusion and ferment of the decade following World War I. On religion, for example, he portrays Lee as musing that "he was obliged to maintain an endless hypocrisy about the miracles, the dogmas and affairs, of Sunday school and the church. As a child he had been so filled with a literal Presbyterian imagery that, when a degree of reason discarded figures of speech seen as concrete actualities, nothing had been left" (89). The author's Freudianism is inexact, but that of other American writers of the Twenties is also. It was the Freudianism, though, that drew strong negative response from contemporary critics such as Henry Seidel Canby, who in his book of essays wrote of "vague desires running wild. . . ."[9] Canby censured the subject matter, such as a worthless country club set, but he lauded the way the author handled the material when he averred that the book "confirms a judgment long held that Mr. Hergesheimer is one of the most skillful craftsmen in English in our day."[10] Other evaluations also objected to Hergesheimer's somewhat frank treatment of the protagonist's urges; but Ludwig Lewisohn, writing in *Nation*, took the opposite view: "Today and for a long period to come it will be more than art—it will be vision, clarification, support to . . . the searching mind."[11] Today Lewisohn's claims of vatic importance for *Cytherea* seem unjustified by the novel's intrinsic worth.

Cytherea is a well-knit story with a number of strengths. There is a joke in the author's reference to an escapade with "John Lenning

Partins," for "John Partins" was the fictional author he used in the
hoax he played in one of his Philadelphia lectures in 1921. Foreshadowing and other technical aspects of the novel are satisfactory.
The symbol of the captive pig is suitable, that of Fanny's angry
blow causing electrical sparks is excellent, as is that of Tanglefoot,
the popular flypaper of the day, but that of the doll strains credulity.
The title itself is appropriate because it implies a love goddess who
brings passionate love which is troubled rather than idyllic.[12] The
fact that Savina, the embodiment of the doll and Cytherean love, has
a weak heart and that she dies from "excesses" is singularly fitting.

Although Hergesheimer told Richard Barthelmess that he regarded
Cytherea as a "serious and tragic" novel (29 December 1921), he
nevertheless wrote to provide entertainment only, as he said to
Lorimer (4 September 1921); and this fact points to a self-imposed
limitation on his novel. *Cytherea* could have profited from a clearer
understanding of the "truth" which Lee thought would free him and,
what is more important, from an injection of significance to the story.
Perhaps Galsworthy showed the most insight when he wished for
greater detachment in the treatment of Lee "so that we felt his place
in the scheme of things, or rather the place of the pathological out-
burst of Leonism from which he suffered, and to which we are all
subject" (29 January 1922). Lee Randon, bemused by a common
phenomenon, seems to be individual rather than representative, and
thus does not stand as a poignant example of what now is called "the
human predicament."

The Party Dress

Complementing *Cytherea* is *The Party Dress* (1930), which appeared first in the *Cosmopolitan* and then in hardback. The point of
view in this continuous-action novel is that of Nina Henry, who is
the counterpart of Lee Randon. In telling her story, the author returns to his practice in *The Bright Shawl* of using no chapters or
main divisions, only a three-asterisk mark.

Pagan love.   Once again Hergesheimer places his story among
the country club set, one of whom is Nina Henry, the wife of a successful executive. She is outwardly happily married, but in the un-
easiness of her early middle age she realizes that she and her husband
Wilson have lost almost all interest in each other. She is flirting

with a wealthy young man named Francis Ambler, and Wilson is pursuing an affair with Cora Lisher, a widow. The Henrys have a son, Acton, and a daughter, Cordelia, both of whom are more sensible than their parents; and Mrs. Lisher has a daughter, Anna Louise. The lives of these people and of others in Eastlake revolve around business, gossip, bridge, parties, and the country club. Into Nina's life comes Chalke Ewing from Cuba, the brother of her neighbor and close friend Mary Gow, wife of a judge. At first Nina is repelled by Chalke, who drinks rum swizzles immoderately and who is a well-read idealist. She wishes to pursue physical love at once, but he insists that they should properly inform Wilson, obtain a divorce, and then get married. On a hot night they go swimming in the nude at the stone quarry, and afterward at home she seduces him. The next day she waits for him to call her, he does not, and she finds he has left for Cuba suddenly. Shortly afterwards at the Gow's engagement party for Anna Louise Lisher and Francis Ambler, Nina learns of Chalke's death—he has killed himself on a train in Cuba, unable to bear his fall from principled behavior. Thus, at the end, Nina is left with a hollow marriage, which will not be improved by the fact that Wilson and Mrs. Lisher have stopped seeing each other.

Analysis and estimate.   The picture of the country club set is vivid, but the mutual affection between Nina and Chalke strains belief. It may be that Hergesheimer intended to stress the power of an irrational Eros in Chalke's attraction to Nina and in hers to him. But she is a nonintellectual who incomprehensibly is pleased by Chalke's erudition and lack of physical attractiveness. Chalke falls too easily to Nina's seductiveness. Perhaps the best stroke in the entire affair is having Chalke, the person with high principles, come from outside the country club set.

Hergesheimer maintains his stylistic mannerisms and resorts to the outworn moth-and-flame symbol, but he adds some new touches that enhance the novel's virtues. He creates the sound of the times with references to popular songs such as "Let's Fall in Love" and "All by Yourself in the Moonlight," and he sensitively describes an owl's cry as "the most hopeless sound in the world."[13] To establish the motif of Aphrodite, Hergesheimer gives Nina a dress by a Parisian designer called Ishtarre, a name derived from the Babylonian goddess Ishtar, later to be called Aphrodite by the Greeks. Best of all he projects Nina's learning of Chalke's death against the background of dance music. He also lets the characters reveal themselves through symbolic actions, such as Nina's long self-indulgent bath each morning.

In his description of women's apparel as of decor Hergesheimer made a shift from aestheticism to a simplicity more in keeping with the times. In *Cytherea* (1922), his next to last novel in the early style, Savina Grove is allotted considerable descriptive detail:

In the close incongruity of this preserved Victorianism Mrs. William Loyd Grove, when she appeared soon after, startled Lee Randon by her complete expression of a severely modern air. She was dressed for the street in a very light brown suit, rigidly simple, with a small black three-cornered hat, a sable skin about her neck, and highly polished English brogues with gaiters. Mrs. Grove was thin—no, he corrected that impression, she was slight—her face, broad at the temples, narrowed gracefully to her chin; her eyes were a darker blue than the velvet; and her skin at once was evenly pale and had a suggestion of transparent warmth. The slender firm hand she extended, her bearing and the glimpse of a round throat, had lost none of the slender flexibility of youth. (150–51)

In *The Party Dress* (1930) the description is much simplified: Nina is seen sitting "on the porch in a new white flannel skirt, a thin black wool sweater, and a chain belt of silver links. There was a black ribbon about her pale half-curly hair, and she had on her best white buckskin low shoes and the sheer stockings she could not be persuaded to vary" (171). Other aspects of style remained substantially the same.

These two novels possess more points in common than any other two of the author's books. They have continuous action, involve suburban life in Eastlake, include a lover's death in Cuba, and achieve an identification of the principal female character with love. They also have excellent foreshadowing but endings that lack inevitability. Perhaps the best part of each is the vivid portrayal of the country club set, a group of frenetic, foolish, and self-destructive suburbanites who toy with sensation and act less sensibly than the prematurely wise teen-agers. As a novel about the Twenties, *The Party Dress* is superior to *Cytherea* in many respects; but in its totality it is less satisfactory because the affair between the uneducated, self-indulgent Nina and the idealistic, erudite Chalke appears incredible.

Hergesheimer's practice of writing novels solely for the reader's pleasure militates against greater worth for these reflections of the "Roaring Twenties." The subject matter is there, but it is not projected against a background that would provide significance to it, even satirically. Many characters seem trivial, it is true; but in *The Great Gatsby* the seekers of frothy sensation are evaluated as contemptible, less worthy of the reader's attention than Gatsby, who after his brief stay at St. Olaf College departed from honesty to make gangster connections so that he could regain Daisy. His story has poignancy, but there can be none if the author does not provide some emotional identification with the characters. Had Hergesheimer put more feeling into his protagonists, their delayed problems of the libido in their forties might have had a more moving importance.

The Foolscap Rose

Hergesheimer's last novel in book form, *The Foolscap Rose*, was written three years after the author had undergone a serious illness in 1930 which affected his creative powers. Published first in the *Saturday Evening Post* (September 1933–May 1934) and then as a book (September 1934) in three sections of three chapters each, it concerns paper-making by a family over many generations in the nineteenth and twentieth centuries.

In his opening scene of paper-making in 1818 Hergesheimer portrays members of the Hazael Wigton family coming from the paper mill to breakfast at the home. Shortly afterward a German Lutheran named Jacob Kinzer stops by, obtains employment, and puts to use the trade he learned in Holland. He is an excellent workman; and, inspired by his love for Rosanna Wigton, he designs a rose-shaped watermark which gives the title to the book. The Wigtons and the Kinzers dominate the story from one generation to the next. One feels Jacob Kinzer's nostalgia for the past when he visits the old mill and sees the mold for the foolscap rose paper, which was dried on felt hung over poles, because for him, "Those with the rest belonged to the days of lost innocence."[14] The second part, in 1879, concerns economic, social, and political changes; and again there is a man exhibiting the steadfastness that the author admired. In the third part (1907) there is a depression, and John Reichardt, another German Lutheran who learned his trade in Holland, joins the firm, marries into the family, and presumably will restore its fortunes.

Analysis and estimate. Hergesheimer, after the comparative

failure of *The Party Dress* with the critics, in this book tried to return
to what he wrote to Knopf was his "proper field" (25 July 1933).
The author created an effective first portion, which he told Cabell he
himself preferred (25 July 1933); but unfortunately he could not
sustain the strong opening and ended with a story that Martin correctly terms "diffuse and disconnected."[15] The negative reaction to
the new novel was so strong that one critic even titled his article
"Who's Loony Now?"[16] The author's loss of creativity caused him
to depend on a set of parallels that contribute unity but are obtrusive;
as a result, the balanced structure and the parallelism between Jacob
Kinzer and John Reichardt seem artificial, and the unexpected shifts
to different partners before marriage becomes annoying. The truth
seems to be that Hergesheimer had lost control of his material in
the days of his waning creativity and was not able to continue his
novel writing about the American past with the success he first
achieved in *The Three Black Pennys*.

"Steel" and "Demeter, A Farm Woman"

Hergesheimer's first novel published in the *Saturday Evening Post*
but not in book form was "Steel," which appeared from 26 June to
31 July 1920. In it he told of an utterly disillusioned returning
soldier, Howard Gage, who came home to his wife at the house of
his uncle, Dan. Howard's father is dead, and Dan hopes that Howard
will enter the steel business, but the young man is not interested in
doing anything after his shattering war experiences. He finds his
wife, Sophie, incredibly frivolous as well as too friendly toward Major
Moreland, a stateside officer courting Dan's young daughter, Charlotte.
As the story unfolds, Dan dies while visiting another steel mill,
Sophie divorces Howard, and he plans to take over the business and
to marry Charlotte.

The story clearly is inferior to the author's novels in hard covers,
but a few points about it are worth noting. In it Hergesheimer captured the lethargic purposelessness of those returning soldiers who
had trouble believing in anything; and he also used again his
research into steel, this time in a modern story. Oddly enough, in
"Steel" as in *The Three Black Pennys*, there are examples of rarely
used humor, in this case involving the smug, poltroonish Major
Moreland. At one time the author was dickering to get the novel
filmed, and he considered rewriting the story for hardback publication

also. In his plans he had an idea that soon became the basis for *Cytherea*. His intention in 1920 was to add to "Steel" a married couple whose male partner in his forties was destroyed by his amorous reaction to the potently charming Charlotte. Fortunately, he did not follow up his planned revision, for "Steel" would have been improved only slightly, and the idea was better exploited in *Cytherea*.

Hergesheimer's last published novel was "Demeter, A Farm Woman," which ran in the *Saturday Evening Post* from 8 August through 12 September 1936. Again the author uses a returned soldier, this one just back from the Civil War. He restores his father's farm to productivity and marries Unity Gow, the taciturn hired girl; but because he is intellect and she is feeling, they lack communication until he realizes she is a person with emotions to be respected. Intermingled with the other story elements are oil speculation and Pennsylvania Dutch witchcraft.

Both "Steel" and "Demeter, A Farm Woman" fall short of the novels published as books. They have the elements from which the author could have constructed solid stories, but the first novel was composed during an intensely busy period, and the second was published after the author's creative spirit had lost its power. Both appeared in the *Post* whose readership was less critical than the book reviewers.

Chapter Eight

Short Stories and Other Prose

In addition to his fourteen novels, Hergesheimer published a substantial amount of other writings. Among them were dozens of short stories, autobiographical writings, biography, belles lettres, travel, and literary criticism. Appearing as individual books, as introductions to books, and as articles or stories in periodicals, they usually are not up to the level of his best novels, but they constitute a revealing and often interesting body of work.

Short Stories

Though Hergesheimer customarily is thought of as a novelist, in his day he also was popularly known as a writer of short stories; and indeed he received most of his income from them. Beginning with "The Professional Game" in 1915 and ending with "The Rose of Lima" in 1941, he turned out over ninety short stories, which appeared most often in the *Saturday Evening Post* but at times in *Redbook*, the *Reviewer*, the *Pictorial Review*, and other periodicals. After magazine publication some of the stories were collected into books: *Gold and Iron*, *The Happy End*, *Quiet Cities*, and *Tropical Winter*. Occasionally a story would be anthologized, as in a volume of "best stories" for a particular year.

"The Professional Game," like the first novel, *The Lay Anthony*, is somewhat amateurish, not up to the standard of following stories; but much improved are the three reprinted in *Gold and Iron* (1918). "Wild Oranges," the first, evokes an irrational terror of nightmarish danger but usually is regarded as less satisfactory than the other two and sometimes as inferior Conrad. Cabell, as well as a few others, though, perceived a distinctive feature of Hergesheimer's narrative technique—his rendering objects as a painter would (12 June 1918). "Tubal Cain" earned plaudits for relating Alexander Hullings's rise to importance in the steel industry, largely through his strength of will. It was "The Dark Fleece," however, that many thought best; and it was the story Hergesheimer mentioned to Mencken in implied self-justification for a collection from a popular magazine (5 April 1918). The story concerns Jason Burrage, newly returned from the California Gold Rush, how he is refused by Olive Stanes because he has killed a man, and how he is accepted by the strong-willed, aristocratic Honora Canderay. The large boulder in the Stanes's yard symbolizes the rock-ribbed family character, which precludes marriage to a Jason returned with a blood-stained fleece. The *New York Times Book Review* and the British W. L. George found the portrait of Honora praiseworthy.[1] Of Hergesheimer's friends, Sinclair Lewis and Cabell sent compliments, but the latter added that Olive would not drop out of Jason's mind so completely that no reference would be made to her in the last part of the story (6 May [1918], 12 June 1918). The three stories also were published individually as books— "Wild Oranges" in 1919 and the remaining two in 1922. Other periodical stories later published as books were "Triall by Armes" in 1929 and "Love in the United States" and "The Big Shot" in 1932.

The Happy End (1919) was the least satisfactory of the collections. Three of the stories are quite unsubstantial, and "Bread" suffers from its ending, in which an overfed August Turnbull dies from the traumatic sight of starved corpses in a boat which fortuitously has drifted into the harbor. "Rosemary Roselle" illustrates the author's affection for the defeated South in the postbellum years; and somewhat better is "The Flower of Spain," a tale of a heroic wife's protection of her husband. Cabell especially liked this story in which Hergesheimer makes one of his few uses of his Italian experiences (11 October 1919). "Tol'able David," which also was published as a separate book (1923) and made into an award-winning movie starring Richard Barthelmess, drew on the author's years in the Virginia mountains. The story tells how the younger son avenges the injury to his older brother and the death of his father against a malicious set of newcomers. Reminding the reader of the three attempts at revenge in folklore, David defeats the trio of evil Hatburns in a fight. Now the story seems naive, but in its day it appealed to the omnipresent unsophisticated audience.

As the omniscient author, Hergesheimer draws an explicit comparison between the biblical hero and the teen-age son of Hunter and Mattie Kinemon. He writes in short sentences with diction generally well suited to the subject, including colloquial mountain words

and expressions such as "right spindling" and "powerful happy." He
uses some of his early ornate style only in the following passage:
"The night swept into the room, fragrant and blue, powdered with
stars; the sheep bells sounded in a faintly distant clashing; a whip-
poorwill beat its throat out against the piny dark."[2] In spite of the
story's popular appeal, Cabell warned that the triumph of good over
evil ran counter to his friend's other work and advised him to reread
the story and engage in penitential prayer (11 & 13 October 1919).
Because Cabell was seriously concerned about what writing for
popular magazines would do to the quality of Hergesheimer's stories,
he cautioned that an author would necessarily have his audience
in mind and unconsciously lower his standards.[3]

In *Quiet Cities* (1928) Hergesheimer returned to evoking the
charming American past, to earlier untrammeled days of self-sacrifice,
principle, courage, and beauty. Before writing, he worked at the
Library of Congress, obtained 170,000 words of notes, and laboriously
sketched out the ten stories. In the first one Thomas Armit represents
the fierce, uncompromising independence and bravery of the early
hunters, who pushed westward in advance of the settlers. In the story
of Martin Van Buren the main character exhibits moral courage
by renouncing a beautiful and wealthy lady to remain on the Union
side; and Andrew Jackson is idolized for his devotion to the memory
of his deceased wife, Rachel. These stories reflect Hergesheimer's desire
to escape from the present, for, as he wrote to a friend, only in
books could he leave the contemporary world.[4] Hergesheimer seemed
satisfied with his stories, but Cabell suggested a lack of polish when
he wrote that the one on Natchez needed a concluding paragraph
telling what Sylvester Dearing was looking at (9 June 1927). Illus-
trating divergent views of *Quiet Cities* are Francis Birrell, who thought
it "absolutely worthless," and Cabell, who called it "magic," his
highest accolade.[5]

A few years later Hergesheimer published his last collection,
Tropical Winter, which satirized materialistic shallowness and its
ironic failures at the time of the Great Depression. When the ten-part
series appeared in the *Post* as "Soirées de Palm Beach" (1931-1932),
only the tenth had a title, "The Roman Villa." After revision, the
entire series was published as *Tropical Winter* (1933). The last
story, given no title in the book, tells of the Roman villa built at
Miami Beach by John Patrick Rock, who had worked his way up
in the steel industry and retired with a fortune. In Miami he is

exploited by the wealthy and talked into building an odd Roman villa with a dining room for sixty, complete with dinner couches. Furthermore, Rock contracts a marriage with a spendthrift divorcée who wastes his money while treating him with contempt.

Both the subject matter and the author's attitude toward it differ from the stories preceding *Tropical Winter* and drew varying reactions. Here Florida and a succession of fatuous people occupy the stage and are satirized, like Rock who can be victimized because of his own folly and social aspirations. Van Vechten wrote enthusiastically that he liked this book better than any other since *Tampico* (n. d.). Clifton Fadiman sarcastically excoriated *Tropical Winter*, but he missed the irony and satire as he developed his contention that Hergesheimer was a writer of the rich: money was the novelist's theology.[6] This point needs explanation, though; for as Alfred Kazin observed in *On Native Grounds*, the rich had entry to the world of beauty, which Hergesheimer sought.[7]

After reading the short stories, one cannot help wishing that the author's goal had been higher than entertainment alone. Had he been so inclined, he could have combined the thought-provoking with the entertaining; and few would doubt that Mencken's best friend was intellectually capable of writing stories of better quality. In at least one respect, though, Hergesheimer judged correctly—the public's taste. And the public bought the magazines whose publishers paid him the most and made possible for the extravagant author not only his bread but also flashy automobiles, a restored house, antique furniture, Stiegel glass, and the writing of novels.

Autobiography

For those interested in following the development of an author, *The Presbyterian Child* (1923), *San Cristóbal de la Habana* (1920), *From an Old House* (1926), and some shorter writings provide valuable facts and insights which help one understand Hergesheimer and his artistic achievement. These publications furnish less the customary autobiographical details and more the development and description of a sensibility. In *San Cristóbal* and *From an Old House* there is much material other than autobiography.

The Presbyterian Child. Though it was published after *San Cristóbal, The Presbyterian Child* deals with earlier years. To Emily Clark's *Reviewer* in Richmond Hergesheimer contributed four nos-

talgic "tintypes"[8] which were well received in the literary world.
Mencken, for example, liked especially those on the grandfather and
the father (11 May 1922). Over forty years old when he was recall-
ing his childhood, Hergesheimer thought that it was not one of
"unadulterated joy."[9] He remembered the sensitive, sickly boy who
was not popular either at the school he attended for a short time or
at summer camps. About the effect on him of such rejection he later
wrote in *The Presbyterian Child*, "No, he wasn't widely cared for,
and his life closed upon itself; it drew its excitements and colors
and longings from what independently his mind and heart discovered"
(46). Though the book records such painful childhood solitude, in
retrospect the author, in a letter to Mencken, recalled the period as
a whole as one "of incredible peace and confidence—of a time when
life appeared to be safe" (9 September 1941). Adding "An Aunt
in Jet" to those sent to the *Reviewer* and changing the titles of two
slightly, Hergesheimer collected his essays into a book which Knopf
published in a handsome autographed edition.

    San Cristóbal de la Habana.   In some respects *San Cristóbal*
is a travel book, but it is more autobiography, as Hergesheimer inti-
mated to his friend Walpole (2 July 1920). *San Cristóbal* states what
the author's sensibility is at the height of his aestheticism, just as
The Presbyterian Child sketched some early factors influencing it.
In this short book about his recent trip to Havana he revealed his
current artistic feelings and the origin of *The Bright Shawl* at the
same time as he depicted the bright colors and mid-Victorian atmosphere of the city.

    Hergesheimer wrote frankly and honestly about himself and his
ideas. He noted that his own emphasis on the moods created by
various settings belonged more to the painter than the writer. Wanting
more freedom in plot, he regretted the novel's limitation to the
probable rather than the possible. He saw the novel as negative rather
than positive because, for him, the protagonist must meet with defeat
and ultimately die. Without any afterlife, the characters achieved
greatness by acting selflessly in a few shining moments with no
thought of reward. If human beings had immortality, he contended,
"the dignity of all the great tragic moments of life and art, the splendor
of sacrifice, was cheapened to nothing."[10] It was the emotional reaction
that concerned him, as he stated when he said he wanted to describe
Havana not as a physical plan but according to his emotional response.
He thought this fact indispensable to his purpose, for he wrote, "If

I couldn't make Havana respond in the key of my intrinsic feelings, if I had no authentic feeling with which to invest it, my book, almost all my books, were a weariness and a mistake" (207).

An example of his aesthetic response is his enjoying watching the beautiful chromatic changes as the sunlight shifted over the stained-glass windows. Being affected by it, he sought to produce not the utilitarian but the ornamental. For those critics demanding realism of writers, he proclaimed he had a different goal—that of producing "a flower spray" (124). He realized that Mencken and Walpole might be right in their warnings against aestheticism, but he delighted in the momentary splendor of a charmingly dressed woman and stated that "it was not what the woman had in common with a rabbit that was important, but her difference. On one hand that difference was moral, but on the other aesthetic; and I had been absorbed by the latter" (206).

A critical problem for Hergesheimer was reconciling his artistry with the taste of the *Post*'s readers. He contended that in his stories points arose that he felt compelled to keep though that action might cause the *Post* to reject the story. As Hergesheimer worded it, "Not that Mr. Lorimer personally had any regard for emasculated chapters, but he was addressed primarily to another integrity than mine; our purposes were not invariably coincident" (156). He did not reconcile the divergent purposes, of course, but prospered from the short stories just as many others did from less artistic novels.

From an Old House.   Both *San Cristóbal* and *From an Old House* are written in the author's clear, direct expository style, but going from the former to the latter is like going from the bright sunshine of midday to the light of late afternoon. Although the latter book was published only five years after the former, the tone is utterly different. Despite his perennial liking for the past, Hergesheimer incorporated a sense of the present and future in *San Cristóbal*; but in *From an Old House* he looks backward in his accounts of the renovation of the Dower House, his philosophy, his ideas on writing, and his withdrawal from a lively social life of a few years earlier. The mood is retrospective.

A substantial part of the book narrates the rebuilding of the house. Hergesheimer fondly tells of his first sight of the structure and something of the early years he and Dorothy spent there. Then comes the decision to renovate and the repeated small crises over maintaining authenticity. The house is a refuge against the noisy

contemporary world, and he loves it so much that he has his station-
ery printed with "The Dower House" at the center top. In addition
he moves an antique desk and table to his downtown office so that
he can draw aid from their association with his home and from their
comforting antiquity.

Hergesheimer reveals himself, too, in his little respect for academic
critics, whom he thought removed from life and given to contro-
versial distinctions, such as that between realist and romanticist. After
spending a period as a visiting author at a university, he felt depressed
because he thought the professors looked down on his writings and
deficient academic training. Uncomfortable in a campus atmosphere,
he enjoyed the company of the local politician Paul McElree and
of men who used quaint speech.

Like many other writers in the postwar period, the author sought
by means of words to reproduce in the reader the same emotional
response the characters had. He wondered whether "it were possible
to put a spring day on paper so that when the page was read all its
sounds and scents would float up and envelop the reader."[11] When
he succeeded in his writing, he thought, he achieved a creation more
real to him than the everyday world or even the Dower House—Lavinia
Roderick's song in *Balisand*, for example (17).

Hergesheimer paid attention particularly to word choice. He strove
for the exact word, but he rejected obsolete ones for his novels of
the past, regarding them as "mere imitation" (74). Emily Clark wrote
that "He has a pure passion for words, their beauty, their ugliness,
and their fitness."[12] This feeling may be partly responsible for the
title *San Cristóbal de la Habana* and for the unusually high propor-
tion of unfamiliar names, such as Saxegotha Laws, Ludowika Winscombe, Jacob Winebiddle, and Pleasant Brinsmede. At times the
names of flowers brought him more pleasure than the flowers themselves: "There were white and mauve garden Pinks, rosy-pink Pinks,
Feverfew and Phlox reddish-violet, carmine-rose, French-purple, white-
rosy-purple Eye and early white. With these were peonies and False
Dragon's Head and English cowslip, cowslips, and blue tufted pansies.
Yes, and two hundred and fifty tulips, Mrs. Moon and Inglescombe. I
would never, from flowers, recapture the delight which enveloped me
with those names" (163–64). As he told Adelaide Neall, his choice
of other names was affected, too, by his reaction to their form and
sound, as for example, Cabeça (de Vaca), which he found romantic,
and Carolana, an early form of Carolina (1 August 1922). The same

artistic sense caused him to advise one aspiring author that *tableaued* was "an outrageous word."[13]

Brief writings. Other autobiographical writings are "Some Veracious Paragraphs," a letter to George Gordon,[14] "Shapes in Light," and the sketch in *Twentieth Century Authors.* In the first he tells of his incredibly poor preparation for writing, his extravagance, his years of rejection slips, and then the earthly rewards gained by his pen. He also lists numerous esteemed authors he cannot tolerate, such as Chaucer; and he mentions a few he admires, among them John Donne. The sketch is much closer to factual autobiography than the previously discussed books. In his long letter to Gordon he gives a rather thorough account of his life and ideas up to November 1918. As one reads it, one is struck by the author's honesty and candor. "Shapes in Light," about his midwinter visit to Hollywood in 1925–26, which is largely factual and mentions Charlie Chaplin and other prominent film names as acquaintances, is a pleasantly written narration. The last sketch, written later in life, is a jaunty account of his life and changes in taste.

At no time does Hergesheimer systematically set forth the facts of his life. To get them, the reader needs to gather them here and there; but perhaps the author did just as well by describing the formative influences on him and his artistic feelings because they record the development of one of America's most popular aesthetic sensibilities.

Biography and Belles Lettres

Several of Hergesheimer's minor books may be grouped in a manner following the author's own classifications as listed on the flyleaf of some of his publications. The first of these is the biographical *Sheridan: A Military Narrative,* and the others are *Swords and Roses,* about the Civil War South, and *Berlin,* something of a travelogue.

Sheridan: A Military Narrative. After a letter from Ferris Greenslet asking about potential interest in doing the biography (3 January 1929), Hergesheimer accepted the assignment and began work on *Sheridan: A Military Narrative* (1931). He found agreeable Greenslet's suggestion that the book be less technical than Sir Frederick Maurice's *Lee the Soldier* and concerned more with the "character and temperament" of the subject (21 February 1929), and he began by reading books and spending weeks doing research in Washing-

ton, D.C. By the summer of 1931, when he was complaining that he
had some difficulty getting access to restricted Sheridan material, he
had divided the book into a foreword and three military panoramas:
"The Mountain," "The Valley," and "The Plain." To these he added
illustrations, maps, a bibliography, and an index.

Hergesheimer aimed at a different kind of biography in striving
"to write an absolutely objective book, bare of all ornament and
especially without the questionable, the heated and partisan, psychological, and physiological romance that today seems so largely
to make up biography."[15] He succeeded in his goal, but he did not
please many readers. He saw a Sheridan who produced victories, accidentally or otherwise, and who was not the gallant, gleaming hero
many thought him to be. On the other hand, Hergesheimer was not in
the debunking school popular at the time.

The book was a failure, as Mencken recognized,[16] probably because of the complexity of the campaigns, the style, and the author's
lack of interest in Sheridan as a character. As an example of style,
a sentence about Sheridan is representative of excessive interruption:
"He was best, most invaluable, at such moments, creating a wild
enthusiasm, an overwhelming self-confidence, in his men."[17] Had
the general as a person been developed more fully, the biography
might have been more satisfactory. It should be remembered, however, that Hergesheimer had difficulty getting access to some material,
perhaps that which Greenslet thought contained new and relevant
information. Whatever the exact cause, *Sheridan* was neither successful biography nor military narrative.

Swords and Roses.   Working with one of the subjects best
suited to his tastes and talents, Hergesheimer evoked an aristocratic
society of the past in *Swords and Roses* (1929). Its heroic men and
lovely ladies had lost the Civil War, and that fact lent a sweet,
melancholy nostalgia to the sketches of the persons included in the
ten-part volume. In his dedication Hergesheimer noted "the simpler
loveliness of the past"; and in accord with that expression, he created
portraits of astonishing heroism in the Southern ladies and military
leaders. Their actions he thought "romantic," interpreting that term as
"a complete agreement between reality and desire."[18]

In this book Hergesheimer used the shorter form that was congenial to him and subject matter he found ideal. After doing considerable research, with the well-paid assistance of Sara Haardt,[19]
he composed ten parts that did not emphasize plot but rather were

permeated with the fragrance of the milieu. But he was not completely satisfied with this book listed as "belles lettres" on a flyleaf, and he stated in a letter to the eminent historian Frederic L. Paxson that he wanted to rewrite the volume in its entirety (4 June 1929). For him "the American Civil War gave aristocratic and lovely women a last transcendent importance; they became the symbol of everything that was priceless in life" (24). And he found the Southern cavalry officers the shining ideal fitting for the Southern women. This was the gallant life of beauty and bravery that Hergesheimer admired. Insisting that only brave men were suited to the role, he rejected General George Pickett when he found the commander stood behind a barn at Gettysburg during the charges.[20]

Such a book drew a mixed reaction. Though Paxson complimented the ease and grace of the style (25 May 1929), Allan Nevins, another noted historian, missed Hergesheimer's intention and thought the book too romanticized and decorative.[21] The leftist crititc C. Hartley Grattan, writing in *Bookman*, found the work insignificant;[22] but Professor Allen Tate, in the *New Republic*, presented a balanced view which pointed out merits, historical errors, and the vagueness of Hergesheimer's "beauty."[23] In sum, this Northern panegyric to Southern figures in the Civil War earned predominantly unfavorable responses and was soon forgotten in the immediacy of Depression problems.

Berlin. Just as "The Magnetic West" in the early 1920s was a different travel record of the United States because it attempted to capture the spirit of the frontier, *Berlin* is a unique travelogue about four central European cities and a Bavarian village. Restricted largely to cafés and pubs and replete with superabundant details in the gustatory record, the book lacks a larger context. Hergesheimer said he did not want to leave a record of merely caviar and beer,[24] but he did that to a great extent, possibly because he was aiming at the audience of the *Saturday Evening Post*, which periodical underwrote the trip. In fact, he said to Mencken that he would have to rewrite his travel record twice, once for the magazine and once for Mencken and himself (1 September 1931).

The chapters are headed Berlin I, Munich, Egern, Vienna, Budapest, and Berlin II. In Berlin Hergesheimer admired the lean, tanned youth; and he began his contrasts between the old order and the new; he thought, for instance, how he would have enjoyed being a Hohenzollern officer in a colorful uniform. Munich he found depressing, but Egern, delightful. Vienna to him was enchanting, as was Budapest.

In all these places he found feminine company who charmed him even when they charged him for a dance or spat fishbones on his sleeve, as did Shiraz, a girl from Iran. But he did not seem pleased with his compatriots, for they were given to such unfriendly acts as whispering about his flirting with Lili in Budapest, for example. Confirming his irritation with American travelers, he told Theodore Roosevelt, Jr. that he intended to write a novel critical of wealthy Americans in southern France when they should be in the United States (9 August 1932).

Paul Horgan wrote Hergesheimer commendations about *Berlin* (30 August 1932), but most critics would agree with R. L. Duffus in the *New York Times*, who at the end of a judicious review asserted that the book ultimately was superficial despite its readable style.[25] Hergesheimer was aware that the book was not profound, of course, but he may have erred in thinking his sketches accurately reflected either the zeitgeist of Mitteleuropa or the tastes of the *Post* readers.

Literary Criticism

Hergesheimer's ideas on writing are found in prefaces, articles, reviews, books, and letters, usually stated directly but never as a succinct credo. Sometimes they are autobiographical, at others they concern the works of other authors. These literary views are valuable as examples of those held by one of the few American aesthetes.

Hergesheimer's basic assumptions were in accord with his emphasis on feeling more than on thought. One of the main points was the primacy of beauty as against utility; as he phrased it, "Roses, in the end, are more important than cabbages."[26] Although he had lost his belief in an afterlife, he had not altered his basic religious outlook on life as a "vale of sorrow," where all people have a lonely way to make on earth.[27] Because life is unsatisfactory and ordinarily dull, literature and the arts can serve a function in addition to pleasure by lifting people out of their daily lives in an expression of ideals and hopes.[28] Though his literary art is always inspired by a woman, an author should avoid physical passion, but at the same time he should be honest and reasonably frank.

The stress on the importance of roses emphasizes only one aspect of beauty as Hergesheimer saw it, for he meant something more than sheer physical loveliness when he stated that Hugh Walpole had the base for "a beauty without which creative writing is empty."[29] What

Hergesheimer had in mind is expressed in his comment that George Moore "couldn't be conscious of the fragile beauty of a flower close against the dark green of its leaves without a wider appreciation of all the fleet, tragic loveliness of life."[30] True beauty, too, meant honesty, a quality he found in the Norwegian novelist Johan Bojer's *The Great Hunger*.[31] Here Hergesheimer emphasized the honesty of the scene in which the youthful Peer Holm and his half sister share a humble meal. In doing this, he stressed the spiritual aspects of beauty rather than the physical, far different from the elaborate decors in novels like *Java Head*.

There were two main subjects for novels, he repeatedly said. The first was the heroic fight against insuperable odds, leading to an ultimate defeat because that is the nature of life. The second is nostalgia for a lost beauty, one which is gone, never to be recovered. Holding these views, he condemned contemporary fiction as "cheap materialism" appealing to the masses.[32] Art, he believed, is aristocratic.[33] The losing fight against great odds probably originated during the theologically upsetting times in which the Higher Criticism and numerous scientific treatises such as *The Origin of Species* and *The Descent of Man* shook the Protestant world to its foundations. Tennyson, Browning, Arnold, and Hardy in England and Edwin Arlington Robinson in the United States were among those who reflected the uncertainty in many sensitive minds. Hergesheimer's reaction lies in his view that the glory of mankind lay in quiet courage before invincible oblivion and in the gesture toward the stars, the movement toward unattainable lost beauty.

In his correspondence with aspiring writers he advocated following simplicity, clarity, the rule rather than the exception, avoiding didacticism and optimism, having self-confidence, and being independent. He urged resorting to the human heart with all its conflicting emotions as the source of stories and he cited George Moore as urging use of the local or provincial to attain the universal.[34] Believing that creative writing could not be taught, he urged novices to develop their own styles and not imitate.

Hergesheimer had little respect for critical opinion because he thought that a review should be encomiastic and because as it usually was written it was "a stupid impertinence."[35] Perhaps for good reason he believed some critics less than thorough because few of them noticed his dropping ornateness beginning with *Balisand*, and several discovered "influences" on him when he thought them nonexistent.

Once he was so exasperated with critics that he made an epistolary release of his wrath to Cabell:

The defects in my books are precisely the defects in me; and I am so besotted as to prefer some of the very worst to many of the excellencies I see in others. Privately I am so damn dumb, so entirely unfitted in equipment to be a creative writer that the persistent fact of my books must have a significance cheerful for me to contemplate. The bearded ladies of the *Tribune* and the petticoated gentlemen of the *New York Times* cannot, I am afraid, discourage me nor abate my not too secret opinion of myself. (27 September 1926)

The concern with critical opinion may have arisen in a sense of insecurity about his novels, and it may also be that his change of style was occasioned by a wish to still the main critical objection.

In twelve reviews, in *Hugh Walpole: An Appreciation,* and in prefaces the author himself offered critical thoughts. In discussing Rudolph von Abele's *Alexander H. Stephens* and Thomas C. Cochran and William Miller's *The Age of Enterprise* he showed competency; but he did his best work on novelists. In his brief monograph on Walpole he sympathetically treated the English author's works and praised him for high artistic standards and basing his novels on the heart. In his introduction to *The Red Badge of Courage* he again stresses the emotional response in lauding Stephen Crane's visualization in the novel.

Hergesheimer's letters give several of his ideas and incisive statements concerning authors, which are valuable because of their frankness and their phrasing. As Van Vechten says in *Between Friends,* "From the point of view of literary value, his letters are easily the best. They are not dashed off. They are created with an eye on posterity."[36] When Sinclair Lewis won the Nobel Prize in literature in 1930, Hergesheimer complimented him on *Babbitt* as well as on his generous attitude toward other authors (10 November 1930). This friendly letter was especially appropriate because Lewis had dedicated *Main Street* to Cabell and his West Chester friend. Of most other authors Hergesheimer had a dimmer view. As he told Mencken, he could not complete reading Dos Passos's *Three Soldiers* (18 October 1921), thought Edmund Wilson's critical encapsulations would cause him "to see a pink wraith of Henry Ward Beecher from Hecate County,"[37] and cited banality in V. S. Pritchett's article on Fitzgerald.[38]

More vivid were his thoughts to Cabell on the revival for the author of *The Great Gatsby*: "Naturally you were engaged by the exhumeters [*sic*] of Scott Fitzgerald, here a whole, suppressed, biography: Scott Fitzgerald could write and didn't; he couldn't drink and did; Zelda, his wife, unable for the dance, writing or floral embellishment of bureaux, had a harder head; he loved her" (11 May 1951). Disliking the academic world, he called literature "the professor's feather-bed,"[39] but he enjoyed Hayakawa's book on semantics. He denigrated Henry Miller's novels: "I am, no less, finished with examples of Miller's style—out of Montgomery Ward by Walt Whitman. . . . Whitman, remember, was the bombastical cowboy of Brooklyn drug-stores."[40] With lively, fluent sentences such as these he maintained his vigorous correspondence, though he was in the minority often enough when judging his contemporaries.

Hergesheimer's appraisal of his own work differed from that made by most critics, especially those who irritated him so much and occasionally were irritated by him. To many he appeared conceited and arrogant, but his reputation as such arose partly from his weak eyes, which prevented his recognizing people more than a few feet away, and from a self-protective role he adopted to prevent psychological wounds.[41] In the privacy of letters he described himself as a serious novelist who did not compromise himself for popularity by including the cheap and dishonest lies which he said sold by the half million.[42] Early in his career he found a common thread in his writings: "Looking back over the whole field of my work a very few things are evident, and principally that I always write about people, men usually near forty, who are not happy. . . . The story at bottom is nearly always the same—a struggle between what is called the spirit and what is called the flesh. The spirit is victorious—that's why it seems to me my books are happy books at the price of all material recognition or success."[43] By and large this passage from 1918 continued to be true. The ethical lessons of the author's youth remained with him.

In its time, when the American public demanded "happy" endings, Hergesheimer's definition ran counter to the usual understanding. W. F. Taylor, for example, believes the overall tone of his novels is different—that it is one of sadness and possibly of tragedy;[44] and

Benjamin Glazer also found the novels filled with a pervasive sadness.[45] There is an autumnal melancholy about Hergesheimer's pages which arises, perhaps, from his keen sense of beauty's transience and his awareness of human mortality. Behind all his work lies his assumption that human life is painfully unjust and susceptible to only moderate improvement, and that "pity" should be the attitude toward mankind's existence.[46]

The sheer volume of Hergesheimer's writings in a relatively short span of years is impressive. Stappenbeck lists 190 contributions to periodicals, most of which were his very popular short stories. His autobiographical works help to explain how an aesthete's sensibility developed. When he tried his hand at biography, he was ill at ease because he was accustomed to selecting impressions rather than marshalling facts. In his belletristic efforts he achieved excellent results in *Quiet Cities* before his illness in 1930, but unsatisfactory ones in *Berlin* after that date. Though he made no pretense of being a literary critic, he repeatedly stated his aesthete's and stoic's creed and, in his last years especially, characterized the work of other authors in brilliant phrases. Neither extensive nor systematized, Hergesheimer's literary criticism is useful for what it reveals of an aesthete's view of the world and of writing.

Chapter Nine

Estimate

Throughout Hergesheimer's writings the reader can see the influences that shaped him and the main ideas that he held. His long years of illness which prevented a systematic education and encouraged self-indulgence, his strong Presbyterian home training, and his years at the art academy visibly affected his work. The impressionistic approach, for example, and the attempt to capture in words the effects gained by Degas with paint are evident throughout his books. In his novels his central ideas are courage in the face of inevitable oblivion and the attraction of lost loveliness. He regarded a life and death according to principle as "happy," but not everyone holds that view, and the many deaths in his stories in addition to the lost beauty give them a somber tone.

The author's conception of beauty is distinctive. Sometimes it appears to be limited to ornate surface detail and elaborate decor; his own statements and practice, though, include character as an essential ingredient of beauty. *Balisand*, one of the better examples of his idea of beauty, contains the surface loveliness of Lavinia and her song as well as the principled conduct of Richard Bale which the author included in his definition.

The air of a daydream customarily pervades the novels. Events fall into place too easily, as they did in Hergesheimer's aforementioned childhood reverie about the lovely young girl coming for him with a coach, rather than as they would in obdurate actuality. In the same way, the foreshadowing often appears not only well done but too well done. If the creative imagination were working from realistic details more closely, not everything would fit with such ease.

The plots, settings, and characters also reflect the author's particular preferences. He wrote most often about men near forty facing a difficult problem and pursuing a single goal without deviation. Plots were not the author's forte, but his settings usually were excellent; and in them he pushed aestheticism to its limits with elaborate decors, as in *Java Head*. In the novels from 1924 on, though, he proved he could diminish the adjectival content and still create atmosphere effectively. In his characters he sought vitality, a quality which was different in women and men. In women it took the form of a thorough, nonassertive charm which makes them attractive adjuncts to masculine achievement. In the males the vitality was exhibited in forcefulness and dominance—as he put it, a "sock in the jaw."[1] The first Howat Penny, Gerrit Ammidon, Richard Bale, Govett Bradier, Chalke Ewing, and several characters in *Swords and Roses*, *Quiet Cities*, and *The Limestone Tree* had the strength and disregard for popular opinion that Hergesheimer found admirable. Whatever the degree of vitality in the characters, he had little interest in them as individuals because he was concerned with the successive generations which he visualized as a flowing river of humanity.

It was his novelistic style that drew most negative criticism. Fortunately he had abandoned the garishness of "Strings and Cylinders" by the time of his first novel, though some "literary" words remained. With *The Three Black Pennys* he discovered his metier and wrote in a style he maintained through *The Bright Shawl*. Then with *Balisand* he dropped the aestheticism objected to by some critics, but he retained the excessive interruption by commas and the coordination or apposition which gave the effect of a painter's touching up a picture with another dab of his brush. Those mannerisms were rare in the author's second style—the one used in *From an Old House*, articles, and letters.

When one looks at the entire corpus of Hergesheimer's novels, he sees that the best work concerns the past. Novels of the present combining the country club and Freudianism accurately reflect their time but lack a pleasing atmosphere as well as a moral background lending significance. *Linda Condon* is modern, but the dominating Neoplatonism makes the present recede into the background. For Hergesheimer the earlier America provided the charming objects stimulating to his imagination and so necessary for a proper emotional effect. From *The Three Black Pennys* to *The Limestone Tree* he did his best writing on the congenial American bygone days, which were amenable to the creation of atmosphere as well as secure, like the Dower House.

A few other points should be made about Hergesheimer's work. First, with unobtrusive ease he handled time's passage. Second, as the 1920s progressed, he grew dissatisfied with the novel as a form because it did not express the multidimensional life he wanted to create on paper. Next, he was extremely sensitive to the sound and form of words, such as the names of people and flowers. And last, his methods of composing were geared more to quantity than to quality. Had he demanded more of himself and revised his novels after they apparently were in completed form, he might well have obtained in the rest of his novels the fortunate results he achieved in *The Limestone Tree*.

Hergesheimer's rapid rise and sudden decline are reflected in the critical opinion about his work. Mencken and Llewellyn Jones were among the first to recognize his potential. Then from 1919 to 1923 he enjoyed his best reception among the critics, most of whom regarded him as one of the superior novelists of the time. There were qualifications, of course, particularly about descriptive passages and the seeming lack of interest in people as individuals; and some correctly saw an aristocratic emphasis, the tendency which led F. Scott Fitzgerald to call Hergesheimer "the best people's best novelist."[2] From 1924 to 1932 he received mixed reviews, with 1932 the year in which the last two predominantly favorable articles were published.[3]

During the years of Hergesheimer's widest appeal the novel won him esteem among readers at home and abroad, translations of his most popular books appearing in many countries. His foreign reputation was high enough so that a German critic likened him to Flaubert as a stylist and to the Dane Jens Peter Jacobsen for knowledge of background.[4] When Henry Albert Phillips questioned over forty European writers concerning their preference in American writers, they invariably included Hergesheimer in their first five.[5] In the United States his short stories, articles, lectures, stage plays, and movies kept his name before the public steadily. He was known to the great mass of people, but also to a number of the intellectuals such as H. L. Mencken, who relished the stimulating company of his friend from West Chester; and publishers such as Knopf and the British Theodore Byard (successor to Heinemann) praised him extravagantly. In 1924 he was elected to the American Institute of Arts and Letters.[6] The general esteem for Hergesheimer led to his being rated third (Booth Tarkington and Edith Wharton were first and second) among living American novelists in the Bookseller's Poll in 1921[7] and first in the *Literary Digest* poll in 1922. Even as late as 1928 he was ranked tenth in the librarian Asa Don Dickinson's *The Best Books of Our Time 1901–1925*.[8]

After Hergesheimer altered his style to one of less ornateness and critics had more novels on which to base their judgment, a less favorable evaluation began to appear. Henry Seidel Canby, characterizing the author's work as that of an antiquarian, was sparing of praise; but he did allow that "The historian of moods and appearances is valuable in literature."[9] Ludwig Lewisohn asserted that Hergesheimer had not advanced as a novelist after *Linda Condon*,[10] a defensible charge. Vernon Louis Parrington perceived faults in the style and saw the novelist as "something of a poseur" though a sensitive artist.[11] Percy H. Boynton cited Hergesheimer's aristocratic capacity for sensuous enjoyment and realized that the earlier works were superior to the later.[12] By 1936 Walter Fuller Taylor wrote that the West Chester novelist lacked an extra quality that would have elevated his works to the first literary rank.[13] In the 1940s Alfred Kazin maintained that Hergesheimer's devotion to beauty ultimately was suffocating his characters.[14] Perhaps even more indicative of the change in taste was the fact that a 1944 *Saturday Review* poll of contributors omitted both Hergesheimer and Cabell.[15] In 1950 Henry Steele Commager mentioned both Elinor Wylie and Cabell in *The American Mind* but ignored Hergesheimer.[16]

The decline in interest concerning Hergesheimer is reflected also in the lack of scholarly attention to him. Since 1950 only eleven articles have been published, many fewer than the annual number for Hemingway, for example. Only five candidates for the doctorate have chosen him for their dissertations (Napier, 1959; Richard Spalding Leever, 1962; Martin, 1964; Stappenbeck, 1969; and Judith Lampert, 1974). Martin developed his dissertation into a book; and Stappenbeck published an invaluable volume on the holdings in the Hergesheimer Collection at the Humanities Research Center, University of Texas (Austin).

One of the few American aesthetes, Hergesheimer ranks among those who filled a void between the novelists prominent before World War I and those of the postwar generation who reflected the traumatic spiritual wound inflicted on the nation. He was not a transitional figure in the ordinary sense because he and the other aesthetes began no school and had no followers. Soon the reading public preferred Hemingway, Fitzgerald, Faulkner, Dos Passos, John Steinbeck, and others of a younger generation; and the Great Depression made novels without a social emphasis seem frivolous compared to the hard urgency of survival.

In the 1980s the significance of Hergesheimer is largely historical. New doctors of American Literature plead ignorance of him, and contemporary writers do not consult him or the other aesthetes for inspiration. The American taste has leaned toward realism; and if people prefer escapism, they often read science fiction. In a world of violence and discord readers have thought that aestheticism lacks relevance and that plot is not to be neglected. For the present, the aesthetes appear as exotics; and it is likely they will continue to seem so. But they bequeathed a legacy of light reading, among the best of which are Hergesheimer's *The Three Black Pennys, Java Head, Linda Condon*, and *The Limestone Tree.*

Notes and References

Chapter One

1. "America's Literary Stars," *Literary Digest* 74 (22 July 1922):28.
2. Herb Stappenbeck, comp., *A Catalogue of the Joseph Herge-sheimer Collection at the University of Texas* (Austin: University of Texas, 1974), pp. 7–8 (Introduction).
3. "The City of Pleasure: Five Impressions," *Forum* 49 (June 1913):734–39; "Five Profiles," *Forum* 50 (Sept. 1913):353–58; "In Strings and Cylinders," *Forum* 50 (Nov. 1913):700–704.
4. Scott Fitzgerald to James Branch Cabell, 4 Mar. 1922 in Padraic Colum and Margaret Freeman Cabell, eds., *Between Friends, Letters of James Branch Cabell and Others* (New York, 1962), p. 251; hereafter cited as *Between Friends*.
5. Burton Rascoe, "Joseph Hergesheimer, a Writer Who Can Converse; and Sherwood Anderson, a Writer Who Can Spin Yarns," in "Contemporary Reminiscences," *Arts and Decoration* 21 (Aug. 1924):36.
6. *From an Old House*, 2d ed. (New York, 1926), p. 187.
7. Carl Van Vechten, "How I Remember Joseph Hergesheimer," *Yale University Library Gazette* 22, no. 3 (Jan. 1948):91.
8. Burton Rascoe, *Before I Forget* (New York, 1937), p. 410.
9. Sara Haardt, "Joseph Hergesheimer's Methods," *Bookman* 69 (June 1929):398.
10. See Julian Boyd to Hergesheimer, 11 and 18 Aug. 1947, Joseph Hergesheimer Collection, Humanities Research Center, University of Texas at Austin (letters cited hereafter are in the Hergesheimer Collection unless otherwise indicated).
11. Alfred A. Knopf, "Reminiscences of Hergesheimer, Van Vechten, and Mencken," *Yale University Library Gazette* 24, no. 4 (Apr. 1950):150.
12. See Hergesheimer to Sinclair Lewis, 22 Apr. 1922, Sinclair Lewis Collection, Collection of American Literature, Beinecke Rare Book and Manuscript Library, Yale University.
13. "The Feminine Nuisance in American Literature," *Yale Review* 10 (July 1921):718.
14. Irene and Allen Cleaton, *Books and Battles: American Literature, 1920–1930* (Boston: Houghton Mifflin Co., 1937), p. 94.

15. Rosalind C. Lohrfinck to Mrs. Dorothy Hergesheimer, 3 May 1954. See also Carl Bode, *Mencken* (Carbondale, Ill., 1969), p. 333. The H. L. Mencken Room at the Enoch Pratt Free Library, Baltimore, houses thirty-four Hergesheimer volumes. The Humanities Research Center has 396 letters from Mencken to Hergesheimer over a thirty-year period.

16. Edward L. Tucker, "Joseph Hergesheimer to Mr. Gordon: A Letter," *Studies in American Fiction* 6, no. 2 (Autumn 1978):220–21.

17. *From an Old House*, p. 141.

18. See Hergesheimer to Mary Scott (Mrs. Everinghim Blake), 7 Sept. 1952, Joseph Hergesheimer Collection (# 7702), Clifton Waller Barrett Library, University of Virginia Library.

19. James Joseph Napier, "Joseph Hergesheimer: A Critical Study" (Ph.D. diss., University of Pennsylvania, 1959), p. 10.

20. Tucker, "Hergesheimer to Mr. Gordon," p. 221.

21. To Norman Bel Geddes, [1950].

22. Napier, "Hergesheimer," p. 11.

23. Introduction to *The Red Badge of Courage* by Stephen Crane, *The Work of Stephen Crane*, Wilson Follett, ed., 12 vols. (New York, 1925), 1:xi.

24. ["The Profession of Imaginary Letters"], complete MS, n. d. (ca. 1914).

25. Emily Clark, *Innocence Abroad* (New York, 1931), p. 95.

26. Henry Albert Phillips, "A Novelist's Uphill Road," *World Today* 52 (July 1928):153.

27. Benjamin F. Glazer, "A New and Dominant Figure in American Letters," *Philadelphia Press Sunday Magazine* [ca. 1919].

28. Napier, "Hergesheimer," p. 16.

29. *From an Old House*, p. 151.

30. See Hergesheimer to Mary Clare Albert, 12 Mar. 1913.

31. 22 Mar. 1917, Sinclair Lewis Collection.

32. To Cabell, 15 June 1918.

33. See Hergesheimer to Barrett H. Clark, 8 Nov. 1928.

34. To Mr. Dorrance, 8 Aug. 1920, Joseph Hergesheimer Collection (# 7702), Clifton Waller Barrett Library, University of Virginia Library.

35. Preface to *Domnei: A Comedy of Woman-Worship*, by James Branch Cabell (New York, 1920), p. 6.

36. Critique on "The Great Hunger," in *Johan Bojer: The Man and His Works*, Carl Gad, ed. (New York, 1920), p. 242. (Appendix).

37. Tucker, "Hergesheimer to Mr. Gordon," p. 222.

Chapter Two

1. Stappenbeck, *A Catalogue of the Hergesheimer Collection*, p. 249.

2. "Fantoccini," *General Magazine and Historical Chronicle* 47 (Summer 1945):209.

3. *The Lay Anthony* (New York, 1914), p. 61; hereafter page references cited in the text.

4. Earl E. Fisk to Hergesheimer, 9 Nov. 1946, Hergesheimer's inscription in a copy of *The Lay Anthony*.

5. William Lyon Phelps to Hergesheimer, 4 Apr. 1919.

6. H. L. Mencken, review of *The Lay Anthony* in *Smart Set* 44 (Dec. 1914):307–8.

7. Llewellyn Jones, review of *The Lay Anthony* in *Chicago Evening Post*, 21 Aug. 1914.

8. T. S. Matthews, "Narcissa Baddery (How to hergesheimer [*sic*] in one easy lesson)," *New Republic* 55 (23 May 1928):20–21.

9. "Some Veracious Paragraphs," *Bookman* 48, no. 1 (Sept. 1918):11.

10. "In Strings and Cylinders," *Forum* 50 (Nov. 1913):700.

11. *Mountain Blood*, 2d ed. (New York:Alfred A. Knopf, 1919), p. 112; hereafter page references cited in the text.

12. *From an Old House*, p. 140.

13. James Branch Cabell, "In Respect to Joseph Hergesheimer," *Bookman* 50 (Nov.–Dec. 1919):269.

14. Review of *Mountain Blood* by Joseph Hergesheimer in *Times* (London), 20 Jan. 1922; in *Nation* 100 (17 June 1915):685; by Mitchell Kennerley in *New York Times*, 30 May 1915, p. 206.

Chapter Three

1. 20 June 1919, *Between Friends*, p. 120.

2. 22 Mar. 1917, Sinclair Lewis Collection.

3. *The Three Black Pennys* (New York, 1930), p. x; hereafter page references cited in the text.

4. "Art," *American Mercury* 9 (Nov. 1926):257.

5. 27 May 1918, *Between Friends*, p. 53.

6. Tucker, "Hergesheimer to Mr. Gordon," p. 219.

7. Carl Van Doren, "Contemporary American Novelists," *Nation* 112 (25 May 1921):742.

8. Clifton Fadiman, "The Best People's Best Novelist," *Nation* 136 (15 Feb. 1933):177.

9. J. C. Squire, *Contemporary American Authors* (New York: Henry Holt & Co., 1928), p. 197.

10. James Branch Cabell, *Joseph Hergesheimer: An Essay in Interpretation* (Chicago, 1921), p. 9.

11. See Hergesheimer to John [Hemphill], 6 Nov. 1917.

12. "A Novel a la Mode," *New Republic* 12 (20 Oct. 1917):334.

13. H. W. Boynton, "Peak and Valley," *Bookman* 46 (Dec. 1917): 487.

14. Vernon Lewis Parrington, *Main Currents in American Thought*, vol. 3 (New York, 1930), p. 380.

15. This information is contained in a letter made available through the courtesy of Mr. Dallett Hemphill, Attorney at Law.

16. W. L. George, "Joseph Hergesheimer," *Bookman* (London) 58 (Sept. 1920):193.

Chapter Four

1. See Hergesheimer to Grant Overton, literary editor, n. d., Collection of American Literature, Beinecke Rare Book and Manuscript Library, Yale University. Overton used the information in his book *Why Authors go Wrong* (1919; reprint ed., Freeport, N.Y.: Books for Libraries Press, 1968), pp. 187–89.

2. "Scholasticus in se Scholia Facit Or, *Java Head* Revisited," *Princeton University Library Chronicle* 3, no. 2 (Feb. 1942):52.

3. Ibid., p. 53. From the notes he also drew a factual article called "Notes for a Blue Water Novel," *Bookman* 48 (Jan. 1919):517–24.

4. *Java Head* (New York, 1919), p. 71; hereafter page references cited in the text.

5. "Scholasticus," p. 54.

6. Glazer, "A New and Dominant Figure," *Philadelphia Press Sunday Magazine* [ca. 1919].

7. Van Vechten, "How I Remember Joseph Hergesheimer," p. 91.

8. Elliot Arnold, an article in *New York Telegram* [ca. 1920].

9. To Van Vechten, 23 Mar. 1918, Carl Van Vechten Collection, Collection of American Literature, Beinecke Rare Book and Manuscript Library, Yale University.

10. "Scholasticus," p. 55.

11. Carl Van Doren, "East and West," *Saturday Review* (London) 128 (Oct. 1919):344.

12. Joseph Warren Beach, *The Twentieth Century Novel: Studies in Technique* (New York, 1932), p. 284; Arthur Hobson Quinn, *American Fiction: An Historical and Critical Survey* (New York, 1936), p. 616.

13. Parrington, *Main Currents in American Thought*, pp. 379–80 (Addenda).

14. Walter Fuller Taylor, *A History of American Letters* (Boston, 1936), pp. 425, 429.

15. Henry Steele Commager, "Glory that was Salem; Based on *Java Head,*" *Scholastic* 57 (8 Nov. 1950):14–15.

16. 6 Jan. 1919, *Between Friends,* p. 98.

17. 18 Apr. 1920, ibid., p. 170.

18. See Hergesheimer to Dr. Phelps, 14 Apr. 1919, William Lyon Phelps Collection, Collection of American Literature, Beinecke Rare Book and Manuscript Library, Yale University.

Chapter Five

1. See Hergesheimer to Van Vechten, 11 Feb. 1919, Carl Van Vechten Collection.

2. "A Dedicatory Note for 'Linda Condon,'" *Everybody's Magazine* 40 (May 1919):43.

3. Rascoe, "Joseph Hergesheimer," p. 36.

4. "A Dedicatory Note," p. 43.

5. Rascoe, "Joseph Hergesheimer," p. 36.

6. *Linda Condon* (New York, 1919), p. 31; hereafter page references cited in the text.

7. "A Dedicatory Note," p. 43.

8. Baldesar Castiglione, *The Book of the Courtier*, trans. and ed. French Simpson (New York: Frederick Ungar Publishing Co., 1959), p. 93.

9. Parrington, *Main Currents in American Thought*, p. 380.

10. To Van Vechten, 25 Apr. 1919, Carl Van Vechten Collection.

11. The typescript in the Van Vechten Collection has this title.

12. George, "Joseph Hergesheimer," p. 193; Joseph Priestley, "Joseph Hergesheimer, an English View," *Bookman* 63 (May 1926):279.

13. "Linda Condon," *Outlook* 123 (31 Dec. 1919):395; "Three Careers," *Nation* 109 (29 Nov. 1919):693; *"Linda Condon,"* *New York Times Review of Books*, 9 Nov. 1919, p. 630.

14. Conrad Aiken, "Two American Novelists," *Athenaeum* 2 (12 Dec. 1919):1339.

15. Carl Van Doren, "Linda Condon," *Spectator* (London) 125 (18 Sept. 1920):371.

16. Napier, "Hergesheimer," p. 99.

Chapter Six

1. To Emma Gray, 23 Apr. 1924, Emma Gray Trigg Correspondence (# 5557–a), Manuscripts Department, University of Virginia Library.

2. See Hergesheimer to William Patten, 31 Mar. 1931.

3. *Balisand* (New York, 1924), p. 41; hereafter page references cited in the text.

4. Percy H. Boynton, *More Contemporary Americans* (Chicago: University of Chicago Press, 1927), p. 142.

5. Hunter Stagg, "About Books," *Reviewer*, 4, no. 5 (Oct. 1924): 415.

6. To Emma Gray, Dec. 1923, Manuscripts Department, University of Virginia Library.

7. Stagg, "About Books," pp. 413–15.

8. "Mr. Hergesheimer gets back to the Post-Revolutionary Period," *New York Times Book Review Supplement*, 14 Sept. 1924, p. 4.

9. Stagg, "About Books," p. 416.

10. Carl Van Doren, "The Tragic Aristocrat," review of *Balisand*, *New York Herald Tribune*, 21 Sept. 1924.

11. Priestley, "An English View," p. 279.

12. To Desha Breckenridge, 31 May 1927.

13. To Lorimer, 21 Nov. 1928.

14. *The Limestone Tree* (New York, 1931), p. 314; hereafter page references cited in the text.

15. See Hergesheimer to Lorimer, 1 July 1927; 21 Nov. 1928; 27 Dec. 1928; 10 Sept. 1929.

16. Joseph T. Shipley, *Dictionary of World Literary Terms*, rev. and enl. ed. (Boston: The Writer, 1970), p. 218.

17. Haardt, "Joseph Hergesheimer's Methods," p. 402.

18. Ronald E. Martin, *The Fiction of Joseph Hergesheimer* (Philadelphia, 1965), p. 168.

19. "*The Limestone Tree*," *Times Literary Supplement* (London), 26 Mar. 1931, p. 250.

20. Fanny Butcher, review of *The Limestone Tree* in *Chicago Daily Tribune*, 3 Jan. 1931.

21. Napier, "Hergesheimer." p. 196.

22. Louis Kronenberger, "*The Limestone Tree*," *Bookman* 73, no. 1 (Mar. 1931):76.

23. "*The Limestone Tree*," *Times Literary Supplement*, 26 Mar. 1931, p. 250.

24. See Knopf to Hergesheimer, 7 Feb. 1951; planned for 23 July 1951 but not reissued.

Chapter Seven

1. *The Bright Shawl* (New York, 1922), p. 214; hereafter page references cited in the text.

2. Joseph Wood Krutch, "The Color of Hergesheimer," *Nation* 115 (22 Nov. 1922):553.

3. H. L. Mencken, "The Monthly Feuilleton," *Smart Set* 69, no. 4 (Dec. 1922):138.

4. Christopher Ward, "Joseph and the Bright Shawl," in *The Triumph of the Nut and Other Parodies* (New York: Henry Holt & Co., 1923), p. 74.

5. See Hergesheimer to J. J. Crespo, 22 Apr. 1925.

6. Martin, *The Fiction of Joseph Hergesheimer*, p. 189.

7. *Tampico* (New York, 1926), p. 22.

8. *Cytherea* (New York, 1922), p. 358; hereafter page references cited in the text.

9. Henry Seidel Canby, *Definitions: Essays in Contemporary Criticism* (New York, 1922), p. 219.

10. Ibid., p. 222.

11. Ludwig Lewisohn, "Review of Cytherea," *Nation* 114 (8 Feb. 1922):176.

12. Ibid.

13. *The Party Dress* (New York, 1930), p. 275; hereafter page references cited in the text.

14. *The Foolscap Rose* (New York, 1934), p. 100.

15. Martin, *The Fiction of Joseph Hergesheimer*, p. 164.

16. T. S. Mathews, "Who's Loony Now?" *New Republic* 81 (12 Dec. 1934):136.

Chapter Eight

1. *New York Times*, 21 Apr. 1918, p. 188; W. L. George, "Joseph Hergesheimer," *Bookman* (London) 58 (Sept. 1920):193.

2. *Tol'able David* (New York, 1923), p. 31.

3. Cabell, "In Respect to Joseph Hergesheimer," p. 270.

4. To Claude Bragdon, 26 June 1928.

5. Francis Birrell, "Reviews," *Nation & Athenaeum* 44 (6 Oct. 1928):19; Cabell, "About One and Another," in *Some of Us: An Essay in Epitaphs* (New York, 1930), p. 6.

6. Fadiman, "The Best People's Best Novelist," p. 177.

7. Alfred Kazin, *On Native Grounds* (New York: Reynal & Hitchcock, 1942), p. 236.

8. "A Scots Grandfather" (Feb. 1922), "An Absentee Father" (May 1922), "With a Cabinet Photograph" (July 1922), and "The Presbyterian Child" (Apr. 1923).

9. *The Presbyterian Child* (New York: Alfred A. Knopf, 1923), p. 10; hereafter page references cited in the text.

10. *San Cristóbal de la Habana* (New York, 1920), p. 106; hereafter page references cited in the text.

11. *From an Old House* (New York, 1926), p. 120; hereafter page references cited in the text.

12. Clark, *Innocence Abroad*, p. 104.

13. To Joel C. Huber, Jr., 19 May 1940.

14. Charles C. Baldwin, "Joseph Hergesheimer," *The Men Who Make Our Novels* (New York, 1919), pp. 36–40; Tucker, "Hergesheimer to Mr. Gordon," pp. 220–24.

15. To W. L. Phelps, 17 Mar. 1932.

16. H. L. Mencken, "Mencken on Hergesheimer," *Baltimore Sun*, 2 May 1954; see also H. L. Mencken, "A Novelist on Furlough," *American Mercury* 27, no. 106 (Oct. 1932):251–54.

17. *Sheridan: A Military Narrative* (Boston, 1931), p. 16.

18. *Swords and Roses* (New York and London, 1929), p. 24; hereafter page references cited in the text.

19. William Manchester, *The Sage of Baltimore* (London: A. Melrose, 1952), p. 195.

20. Haardt, "Joseph Hergesheimer's Methods," p. 399.

21. See Allan Nevins to Knopf, 20 Apr. 1929.

22. C. Hartley Grattan, review of *Swords and Roses* in *Bookman* 69 (May 1929):325–26.

23. Allen Tate, review of *Swords and Roses* in *New Republic* 59 (29 May 1929):50–51.

24. *Berlin* (New York, 1932), p. 187.

25. R. L. Duffus, "Joseph Hergesheimer on Mitteleuropa: An American Novelist's Wayfaring from Berlin's Beer Halls to the Bavarian Mountains," *New York Times Book Review Section*, 24 July 1932, p. 2.

26. *Hugh Walpole: An Appreciation* (New York, 1919), p. 31.

27. "A Dedicatory Note for 'Linda Condon,'" *Everybody's Magazine*, p. 43.

28. "Another Aiken Paper: How, in the Sound of an After Dinner Song, the Novelist Found the Significance of His Art," *Vanity Fair* 16 (Aug. 1921):24.

29. *Hugh Walpole*, p. 3.

30. "George Moore," *New York Evening Post Literary Review* 4 (15 Dec. 1923):362.

31. Critique on "The Great Hunger," p. 242.

32. *Hugh Walpole*, p. 26.

33. "The Profession of Novelist," in *The Novel of Tomorrow* by Twelve American Novelists (Indianapolis, 1922), p. 83.

34. See Hergesheimer to Van Vechten, 7 June 1917.

35. To Cabell, 30 Sept. 1919.

36. *Between Friends*, p. x (Introduction).
37. To Huntington [Cairns], n. d.
38. See Hergesheimer's draft to Huntington Cairns, n. d.
39. Draft to Jack Dalton, n. d.
40. To Huntington Cairns, 30 Nov. 1939.
41. See Phoebe H. Gilkyson, "Joseph Hergesheimer: An Appreciation," *Daily Republican*, Phoenixville, Pa., 3 May 1954.
42. See Hergesheimer to John Robinson, 8 June 1918.
43. Tucker, "Hergesheimer to Mr. Gordon," p. 221.
44. See Taylor, *A History of American Letters*, p. 425.
45. Benjamin F. Glazer, "A New and Dominant Figure," *Philadelphia Press Sunday Magazine* [ca. 1919].
46. "The Lamentable Trade of Letters," *American Mercury* 25 (Mar. 1932):268.

Chapter Nine

1. *From an Old House*, p. 47.
2. Sara Mayfield, *The Constant Circle: H. L. Mencken and His Friends* (New York, 1968), p. 6.
3. Napier, "Hergesheimer," pp. 257, 262.
4. Friedrich Bruns, *Die Americanische Dichtung Der Gegenwart* (Leipzig und Berlin: B. G. Teubner, 1930), p. 41.
5. Henry Albert Phillips, "A Novelist's Uphill Road," *World Today* 52 (July 1928):154.
6. James Branch Cabell, *Straws and Prayer-books* (New York, 1924), p. 209.
7. *Publisher's Weekly* Bookseller's Poll, 24 Sept. 1921 in Jay B. Hubbell, *Who are the Major American Writers?* (Durham, N. C., 1972), pp. 210–11.
8. Hubbell, ibid., p. 293.
9. Henry Seidel Canby, "Too Soon—and Too Late," *American Estimates* (New York: Harcourt, Brace & Co., 1929), pp. 282–87.
10. Ludwig Lewisohn, *Expression in America* (New York: Harper & Brothers, 1932), p. 505.
11. Parrington, *Main Currents in American Thought*, p. 379.
12. Percy H. Boynton, *Literature and American Life* (New York: Ginn & Co., 1936), pp. 794, 796.
13. Taylor, *A History of American Letters*, p. 429.
14. Kazin, *On Native Grounds*, p. 237.
15. Hubbell, *Who Are the Major American Writers?*, pp. 225–26.
16. Henry Steele Commager, *The American Mind* (New Haven: Yale University Press, 1950), pp. 116–19.

Selected Bibliography

PRIMARY SOURCES

1. Novels (books)

Balisand. New York: Alfred A. Knopf, 1924.

The Bright Shawl. New York: Alfred A. Knopf, 1922.

Cytherea. New York: Alfred A. Knopf, 1922.

The Foolscap Rose. New York: Alfred A. Knopf, 1934.

Java Head. New York: Alfred A. Knopf, 1919.

The Lay Anthony. New York and London: Mitchell Kennerley, 1914.

The Limestone Tree. New York: Alfred A. Knopf, 1931.

Linda Condon. New York: Alfred A. Knopf, 1919.

Mountain Blood. New York: Mitchell Kennerley, 1915.

The Party Dress. New York: Alfred A. Knopf, 1930.

Tampico. New York: Alfred A. Knopf, 1926.

The Three Black Pennys. New York: Alfred A. Knopf, 1917. 2d ed. New York: Alfred A. Knopf, 1930.

2. Novels (in periodical)

"Demeter, A Farm Woman." *Saturday Evening Post* (henceforth abbreviated as *SEP*) 209 (8 Aug. 1936):8.

"Steel." *SEP* 192 (26 June 1920):3.

3. Short Stories (books)

Gold and Iron. New York: Alfred A. Knopf, 1918 (comprised of "Wild Oranges," "Tubal Cain," and "The Dark Fleece." All were published separately, the first in 1919 and the others in 1922, by Alfred A. Knopf.)

The Happy End. New York: Alfred A. Knopf, 1919. (Contains "Lonely Valleys," "The Egyptian Chariot," "The Flower of Spain," "Tol'able David," "Bread," "Rosemary Roselle," and "The Thrush in the Hedge." "Tol'able David" was published in book form in 1923 by Alfred A. Knopf).

Love in the United States and The Big Shot. London: Ernest Benn, 1932. "New Ninepenny Novels" No. 21.

Quiet Cities. New York: Alfred A. Knopf, 1928.
Triall by Armes. London: Elkin Mathews & Marrot, 1929. "The Woburn Books" No. 17.
Tropical Winter. New York: Alfred A. Knopf, 1933.

4. Short Stories (in periodicals)
"Bread." *SEP* 191 (30 Nov. 1918):5.
"Changu." *Chicago Sunday Tribune,* 27 June 1920, pp. 1–3.
"Coral." *SEP* 200 (31 Dec. 1927):3.
"The Crystal Chandelier." *SEP* 207 (14 July 1934):12.
"The Dark Fleece." *SEP* 190 (30 Mar. 1918):3.
"The Egyptian Chariot." *SEP* 191 (14 Sept. 1918):9.
"The Flower of Spain." *SEP* 189 (5 Aug. 1916):15.
"Joy Riders." *SEP* 189 (16 Dec. 1916):3.
"Juju." *SEP* 194 (30 July 1931):5.
"Lesbia." *SEP* 188 (31 July 1915):6.
"The Little Kanaka." *Reviewer* 1 (1 May 1921):169–71.
"Lonely Valleys." *SEP* 191 (15 Mar. 1919):13.
"The Meeker Ritual." *Century* 98 (June 1919):145–59.
"The Meeker Ritual: II." *Century* 98 (Oct. 1919):737–51.
"The Professional Game." *SEP* 187 (3 Apr. 1915):20.
"Read Them and Weep." *Century* 99 (Jan. 1920):289–302.
"The Rose of Lima." *Liberty* 18 (25 Oct. 1941):12.
"Rosemary Roselle." *SEP* 189 (30 Sept. 1916):12.
"Scarlet Ibis." *SEP* 193 (13 Nov. 1920):5.
"Sprig of Lemon Verbena." *SEP* 194 (17 Sept. 1921):8.
"The Thrush in the Hedge." *SEP* 188 (10 June 1916):18.
"The Token." *SEP* 194 (22 Oct. 1921):12.
"Tol'able David." *SEP* 190 (14 July 1917):5.
"Tubal Cain." *SEP* 189 (19 May 1917):9.
"Wild Oranges." *SEP* 188 (5 Feb. 1916):3.

5. Nonfiction Books
Berlin. New York: Alfred A. Knopf, 1932.
Biography and Bibliographies. New York: Charles Scribner's Sons, 1931.
From an Old House. New York: Alfred A. Knopf, 1926.
Hugh Walpole, an Appreciation. New York: George H. Doran, 1919.
The Presbyterian Child. London: William Heinemann, 1924.
San Cristóbal de la Habana. New York: Alfred A. Knopf, 1920.
Sheridan: A Military Narrative. Boston: Houghton Mifflin Co., 1931.
Swords and Roses. New York and London: Alfred A. Knopf, 1929.

6. Articles and Sketches

"An Aiken Paper: How the Characters of a Novel, as yet Unwritten, Came Into Being." *Vanity Fair* 16 (July 1921):21–22.

"Another Aiken Paper: How, in the Sound of an After Dinner Song, the Novelist Found the Significance of His Art." *Vanity Fair* 16 (Aug. 1921):23–24.

"Art." *American Mercury* 9 (Nov. 1926):257–63.

"The City of Pleasure: Five Impressions." *Forum* 49 (June 1913): 734–39.

"Fantoccini." *General Magazine and Historical Chronicle* 47 (Summer 1945):203–9.

"The Feminine Nuisance in American Literature." *Yale Review* 10 (July 1921):716–25.

"Five Profiles." *Forum* 50 (Sept. 1913):353–58.

"George Moore." *New York Evening Post Literary Review* 4 (15 Dec. 1923):361–62.

"In Strings and Cylinders." *Forum* 50 (Nov. 1913):700–704.

"James Branch Cabell." *American Mercury* 13 (Jan. 1928):38–47.

"The Lamentable Trade of Letters." *American Mercury* 25 (Mar. 1932): 262–68.

"Letter to Carl Van Vechten." *Bookman* 49 (Aug. 1919):766.

"The Magnetic West." *SEP* 195 (2 Sept. 1922–17 Feb. 1923):3. Nine installments.

"Notes for a Blue Water Novel." *Bookman* 48 (Jan. 1919):517–24.

"The Profession of Novelist." *New Republic* 30 (12 Apr. 1922):14.

"The Return to Reading." *Bookman* 50, no. 1 (30 Sept. 1919):1–3.

"Scholasticus in se Scholia Facit Or, *Java Head* Revisited." *Princeton University Library Chronicle* 3 (Feb. 1942):52–55.

"Shapes in Light." *SEP* 198 (6 Mar. 1926):3.

"Some Veracious Paragraphs." *Bookman* 48 (Sept. 1918):8–12.

7. Parts of Books

Autobiographical sketch in *Twentieth Century Authors*. Edited by Stanley J. Kunitz and Howard Haycraft. New York: H. W. Wilson Co., 1942.

Foreword to *A Bibliography of the Works of Joseph Hergesheimer*, by H. L. R. Swire. Philadelphia: The Centaur Book Shop, 1922.

Foreword to *Five Thousand Years of Vanity*. Philadelphia: The University Museum, January 1944.

Introduction to *Colonial Houses, Philadelphia, Pre-Revolutionary Period*, by Philip B. Wallace. New York: Architectural Book Publishing Co., 1931.

Introduction to *Hagar's Hoard*, by George Kibbe Turner. New York: Alfred A. Knopf, 1925.

Introduction to *Interiors of Virginia Houses of Colonial Times*, by Edith Tunis Sale. Richmond: William Byrd Press, 1927.

Introduction to *The Red Badge of Courage*, by Stephen Crane. Vol. 1. *The Work of Stephen Crane*. Edited by Wilson Follett. 12 vols. New York: Alfred A. Knopf, 1925.

Introduction to *Tales of My Native Town*, by Gabriele D'Annunzio. New York: Doubleday, Page & Co., 1920.

"Mr. Henry L. Mencken." *The Borzoi 1925*. New York: Alfred A. Knopf, 1925.

"A Note on the Chinese Poems Translated by Arthur Waley." *The Borzoi 1920*. New York: Alfred A. Knopf, 1920.

Preface to *Domnei: A Comedy of Woman-Worship*, by James Branch Cabell. New York: Robert M. McBride & Co., 1920.

"The Profession of Novelist." *The Novel of Tomorrow*, by Twelve American Novelists. Indianapolis: Bobbs-Merrill Co., 1922.

Twenty-one letters in *Between Friends: Letters of James Branch Cabell and Others*. Edited by Padraic Colum and Margaret Freeman Cabell. New York: Harcourt, Brace & World, 1962.

8. Reviews

"Alexander H. Stephens: The Specter of Rebellion." *Cleveland News*, 21 Sept. 1946 (a review of Rudolph von Abele's *Alexander H. Stephens*).

"Casanova Passes." *Nation* 113 (14 Dec. 1921):705–6 (a review of Arthur Schnitzler's *Casanova's Homecoming*).

"George Moore." *Literary Review* 4 (15 Dec. 1923):361–62 (a review of *The Works of George Moore*).

"The Great Hunger." *Johan Bojer: The Man and His Works*. Edited by Carl Gad. Translated by Elizabeth Jelliffe MacIntire. New York: Moffat, Yard & Co., 1920.

"Hergesheimer on Conrad's New Novel." *New York Sun*, 13 Apr. 1919, section 7 (a review of Joseph Conrad's *The Arrow of Gold*).

"Hugh Walpole's Cathedral." *Bookman* 56 (Jan. 1923):625–28.

"An Improvisation on Themes from *Jurgen*." *New York Sun*, 26 Oct. 1919 (a review of James Branch Cabell's *Jurgen*).

"The Life and Times of American Business." *Saturday Review of Literature* 25, no. 45 (7 Nov. 1942):5–6 (a review of Thomas C. Cochran's and William Miller's *The Age of Enterprise*).

"Lyrical Mr. George Moore." *Saturday Review of Literature* 1 (3 Jan. 1925):425–26 (a review of George Moore's *Pure Poetry*).

"Magical Stream." *Saturday Review of Literature* 24 (10 May 1941):8
   (a review of Henry S. Canby's *The Brandywine*).
"The Roaring Forties." *Dial* 67 (15 Nov. 1919):431–33 (a review of
   Ralph D. Paine's *The Old Merchant Marine*).
"The Tropics and the White Man." *New York Herald Tribune*, 9 May
   1926, section 7 (a review of Isa Glenn's *Heat*).

SECONDARY SOURCES

1. Bibliographies
Napier, James Joseph. "Joseph Hergesheimer: A Selected Bibliography,
   1913–1945." *Bulletin of Bibliography* 24 (1963–64):46–48, 52,
   69–70.
Stappenbeck, Herb, comp. *A Catalogue of the Joseph Hergesheimer
   Collection at the University of Texas*. Austin: University of Texas,
   1974.

2. Books
Cabell, James Branch. *Joseph Hergesheimer: An Essay in Interpretation*.
   Chicago: Bookfellows, 1921. Superior evaluation.
Jones, Llewellyn. *Joseph Hergesheimer: The Man and His Books*. New
   York: Alfred A. Knopf, 1920. A sympathetic early analysis of the
   writings to 1920.
Martin, Ronald E. *The Fiction of Joseph Hergesheimer*. Philadelphia: Uni-
   versity of Pennsylvania Press, 1965. Indispensable for Hergesheimer
   scholarship.

3. Parts of Books
Adcock, Arthur St. John. "Joseph Hergesheimer." *The Glory that was
   Grub Street*. 1928. Reprint. Freeport, N.Y.: Books for Libraries
   Press, 1969. Perceptive evaluation of the novels.
Baldwin, Charles C. "Joseph Hergesheimer." *The Men Who Make Our
   Novels*. New York: Moffat, Yard & Co., 1919. Early estimate
   drawing on a letter from the author.
Beach, Joseph Warren. "Incoherence in the Aesthete: Mr. Joseph Herge-
   sheimer." *The Outlook for American Prose*. Chicago: University of
   Chicago Press, 1926. Scattered unfavorable comments from a prom-
   inent academic critic.
————. "Point of View: Hergesheimer." *The Twentieth Century Novel:
   Studies in Technique*. New York: Century Co., 1932. Able discus-
   sion of point-of-view in the novels.

Bechhofer, C. E. *The Literary Renaissance in America.* London, William Heinemann, 1923. English evaluation seeing the influence of Conrad and James, and citing stylistic lapses.

Blankenship, Russell. "Joseph Hergesheimer." *American Literature as an Expression of the National Mind.* New York: Henry Holt & Co., 1931. Balanced judgment in a lively style.

Bode, Carl. *Mencken.* Carbondale, Ill.: Southern Illinois University Press, 1969. Valuable sidelights on Hergesheimer, especially his decline.

Boyd, Ernest. "Joseph Hergesheimer." *Portraits: Real and Imaginary.* New York: George H. Doran Co., 1924. Insights into Hergesheimer's writing.

Cabell, James Branch. "About One and Another. A Note as to Joseph Hergesheimer." Chap. 8. *Some of Us: An Essay in Epitaphs.* New York: Robert M. McBride & Co., 1930. Sympathetic, perceptive account by a friend and fellow aesthete.

———. "Diversions of the Anchorite." *Straws and Prayer-books.* New York: R. M. McBride & Co., 1924. Valuable analysis of Hergesheimer's work. Includes *Joseph Hergesheimer: An Essay in Interpretation.*

Canby, Henry Seidel. "Mr. Hergesheimer's *Cytherea.*" *Definitions: Essays in Contemporary Criticism.* New York: Harcourt, Brace & Co., 1922. Praise for Hergesheimer's art and censure of *Cytherea* by a prominent literary figure.

Clark, Emily. *Innocence Abroad.* New York: Alfred A. Knopf, 1931. Correspondence with Emily Clark, largely about the *Reviewer.*

Colum, Padraic, and Margaret Freeman Cabell, eds. *Between Friends: Letters of James Branch Cabell and Others.* New York: Harcourt, Brace & World, 1962. Valuable collection of letters between Cabell and his correspondents.

Farrar, John. "Joseph Hergesheimer." *The Literary Spotlight.* Freeport, N. Y.: Books for Libraries Press, 1924. Articulate analysis of the author and his work.

Follett, Wilson. "Joseph Hergesheimer." *The Borzoi 1920.* New York: Alfred A. Knopf, 1920. Sound analysis stressing the visual aspects of the novels.

Garnett, Edward. "A Note on Two American Novelists: Joseph Hergesheimer and Sherwood Anderson." *Friday Nights: Literary Criticisms and Appreciations.* London: Jonathan Cape, 1922. Praises the achievement in *Java Head.*

Gunn, Drewey Wayne. *American and British Writers in Mexico, 1556–1973.* Austin: University of Texas Press, 1974. Mentions the decline of a once-popular author.

Hartwick, Harry. "Costumes by Hergesheimer." *The Foreground of Amer-*

ican Fiction. New York: American Book Co., 1934. Sees the stories as quests and the beauty as superficial.

Hatcher, Harlan. "Facing Two Worlds: Joseph Hergesheimer." *Creating the Modern American Novel.* New York: Farrar & Rinehart, 1935. Sound evaluation of the author's novels.

Hubbell, Jay B. *Who Are the Major American Writers?* Durham, N. C.: Duke University Press, 1972. Includes a record of Hergesheimer's varying literary standing.

Langford, Gerald, ed. *Ingénue Among the Lions: The Letters of Emily Clark to Joseph Hergesheimer.* Austin: University of Texas Press, 1965. Correspondence about the *Reviewer.*

Levinson, André. "Un Roman D'Aventures: *Tampico* de Joseph Hergesheimer." *Figures Américaines.* Paris and Neuchâtel: Editions Victor Attinger, 1929. A sound French estimate of Hergesheimer's work.

Mayfield, Sara. *The Constant Circle: H. L. Mencken and His Friends.* New York: Delacorte Press, 1968. Lively, gossipy comments.

Millett, Fred B. *Contemporary American Authors.* New York: Harcourt, Brace & Co., 1940. A sound, brief evaluation.

Nathan, George Jean. "Hergy," *The Borzoi 1925.* New York: Alfred A. Knopf, 1925. Comments on Hergesheimer by a prominent New Yorker.

Parrington, Vernon Louis. *Main Currents in American Thought.* New York: Harcourt, Brace & Co., 1930. Brief evaluation by a prominent scholar.

Pattee, Fred Lewis. *The New American Literature 1890-1930.* New York: Century Co., 1930. A basically unsympathetic evaluation.

Quinn, Arthur Hobson. *American Fiction: An Historical and Critical Survey.* New York: D. Appleton-Century Co., 1936. A brief estimate.

Rascoe, Burton. *Before I Forget.* New York: Literary Guild of America, 1937. Praises Hergesheimer as a craftsman.

Taylor, Walter Fuller. *A History of American Letters.* With bibliographies by Harry Hartwick. Boston: American Book Co., 1936. A judicious appraisal.

Tebbel, John. *George Horace Lorimer and "The Saturday Evening Post."* Garden City, N. Y.: Doubleday & Co., 1948. Includes important facts about the Lorimer and *Post* relations with Hergesheimer.

Van Gelder, Robert. "The Curious Retirement of Mr. Hergesheimer." *Writers and Writing.* New York: Charles Scribner's Sons, 1946. Worthwhile report on an interview with Hergesheimer.

Wagenknecht, Edward. "Joseph Hergesheimer: Brocade and Dream." *Cavalcade of the American Novel.* New York: Henry Holt & Co., 1952. A scholarly evaluation of the author's work.

Williams, Blanche. "Joseph Hergesheimer." *Our Short Story Writers.* New York: Dodd, Mead & Co., 1920. Fresh slants on the early short story writers.

4. Articles

Aiken, Conrad. "Two American Novelists." *Athenaeum* 2 (12 Dec. 1919):1339. A perceptive analysis of *Linda Condon.*

Boynton, Percy H. "Joseph Hergesheimer." *English Journal* 16 (May 1927):335–45. Article urging Hergesheimer to write about the aristocratic past rather than the modern clubhouse.

Cabell, James Branch. "In Respect to Joseph Hergesheimer." *Bookman* 50 (Nov.–Dec. 1919):267–73. Many valuable insights by his literary friend.

Canby, Henry Seidel. "Too Soon and Too Late." *Saturday Review* 4 (2 June 1928):925–26. A competent critic sees Hergesheimer as an escapist.

Commager, H. S. "Glory that was Salem; Based on *Java Head.*" *Scholastic* 57 (8 Nov. 1950):14–15. A prominent historian praises Hergesheimer's evocative power.

Fadiman, Clifton. "The Best People's Best Novelist." *Nation* 136 (15 Feb. 1933):175–77. An economic emphasis in an appraisal of the author's work.

Follett, Wilson. "Factualist Versus Impressionist." *Dial* 66 (3 May 1919):449–51. A valuable, perceptive essay on the author's early novels.

Gagnot, Berthe. "Un Romancier Américain." *Revue Anglo-Américaine* 3 (Aug. 1926):505–10. Excellent French appraisal.

George, W. L. "Joseph Hergesheimer." *Bookman* (London) 58 (Sept. 1920):193–94. An early balanced British appraisal.

Haardt, Sara. "Joseph Hergesheimer's Methods." *Bookman* 69 (June 1929):398–403. Useful, firsthand information by a friend.

Justus, James H. "Joseph Hergesheimer's Germany: A Radical Art of Surfaces." *Journal of American Studies* 7, no. 1 (Apr. 1973):47–66. Analysis of Hergesheimer's *Berlin.*

Kelley, Leon. "America and Mr. Hergesheimer." *Sewanee Review* 40 (Apr.–June 1932):171–93. Interesting stress on the author's "American" quality.

Mencken, H. L. "The Niagara of Novels." *Smart Set* 67 (Apr. 1922):138–40. Vigorous defense of Hergesheimer's English and *Cytherea.*

———. "A Novelist on Furlough." *American Mercury* 27 (Oct. 1932):251–54. Forthright remarks about *Sheridan, Berlin,* and *Biography and Bibliographies.*

Napier, James J. "Letters of Sinclair Lewis to Joseph Hergesheimer, 1915–1922." *American Literature* 38 (May 1966): 236–46. Solid demonstration of Lewis's admiration for Hergesheimer.

Phillips, Henry Albert. "A Novelist's Uphill Road." *World Today* 52 (July 1928):151–54. Readable account of a visit to the author at the Dower House.

Priestley, J. B. "Joseph Hergesheimer, an English View." *Bookman* 63 (May 1926):272–80. Valuable observations by a discerning British novelist.

Rascoe, Burton. "Joseph Hergesheimer, a Writer Who Can Converse; and Sherwood Anderson, a Writer Who Can Spin Yarns." *Arts and Decoration* 21 (Aug. 1924):36, 66–67. Interesting, informative essay on the author's personality and work.

———. "The Literary Spotlight VIII; Joseph Hergesheimer." *Bookman* 55 (May 1922):247–51. A somewhat unfavorable analysis of the author's life and stories.

Tucker, Edward L. "Joseph Hergesheimer to Mr. Gordon: A Letter." *Studies in American Fiction* 6, no. 2 (Autumn 1978):218–27. The accurate, full text of Hergesheimer's autobiographical letter to Charles C. Baldwin.

Van Doren, Carl. "Contemporary American Novelists." *Nation* 112 (25 May 1921):741–42. A favorable estimate by a respected academic critic.

Van Vechten, Carl. "How I Remember Joseph Hergesheimer." *Yale University Library Gazette* 22 (Jan. 1948):87–93. Invaluable personal insights by a close friend.

Wagenknecht, Edward. "Our Changing Literary Temper." *English Journal* 34 (May 1945):235–42. Interesting argument that the dichotomy between past and present led to the end of the novelist's career.

Walpole, Hugh. "Contemporary American Fiction." *Independent* 110 (14 Apr. 1923):248–49. An English novelist argues that the American novel has become independent.

West, Geoffrey. "Joseph Hergesheimer, an Appreciation." *English Review* 53 (Oct. 1931):556–64. A sympathetic essay explaining the author's writing about the past.

5. Dissertation

Napier, James Joseph. "Joseph Hergesheimer: A Critical Study." Ph.D. Dissertation, University of Pennsylvania, 1959. Excellent thesis which utilizes personal interviews with the author.

Index

Aiken, Conrad, 52, 53
American Mind, The (Commager), 100
"Annot in the World," 12
Arrow of Gold (Conrad), 48
"Artist of the Beautiful, The" (Hawthorne), 53

Babbitt (Lewis), 30, 94
Baldwin, Charles C. [pseud, George Gordon], 89
Balisand: analysis and estimate, 57–61, 67; introduction, 54–55; mentioned, 2, 9, 10, 61, 73, 88, 93, 97, 98; the story, 55–57
Barthelmess, Richard, 4, 32, 70, 76
Beach, Joseph Warren, 43
Bennett, Arnold, 26
Berlin: mentioned, 5, 7, 89; synopsis and analysis, 91–92, 96
Best Books of Our Time 1901–1925, The (Dickinson), 99
Between Friends: Letters of James Branch Cabell and Others (Colum and Cabell), 94
Bojer, Johan, 93
Book of the Courtier, The (Castiglione), 49
Boyd, Julian, 4
Boynton, H. W., 31
Boynton, Percy H., 57, 100
"Bread," 83
Bright Shawl, The: analysis and estimate, 69–70; introduction, 68; mentioned, 2, 54, 86, 98; the story, 68–69
Butcher, Fanny, 65
Byard, Theodore, 99

Cabell, James Branch: aesthete, 1, 9, 10, 37, 43; critic, 14, 15, 19, 21, 29, 38, 43, 44, 82, 83, 84; mentioned, 3, 4, 5, 10, 22, 52, 57, 59, 62, 80, 94, 95, 100
Cairns, Huntington, 4
Canby, Henry Seidel, 100
Castiglione, Baldesar, 49
Clark, Arthur H., 33, 35
Clark, Emily, 3, 4, 57, 85, 88
Cleeve, Lucas. *See* Kingscote, Mrs. Adelina, 2, 12
Commager, Henry Steele, 43; *The American Mind*, 100
Conrad, Joseph, 6, 7, 32, 48, 66, 82; *Arrow of Gold*, 48; *Nostromo*, 7; *Youth*, 7
Cormack, Bartlett, 71
Cosmopolitan, 76
Crane, Stephen, 7, 94; *The Red Badge of Courage*, 7, 94
Cytherea: analysis and estimate, 75–76, 78, 79; introduction, 74; mentioned, 2, 54, 68, 73, 76, 81; the story, 74–75

"Dark Fleece, The," 9, 83
"Demeter, a Farm Woman," 68, 81
Dickinson, Asa Don, 99
Dos Passos, John, 5, 94, 100; *Three Soldiers*, 94
Duffus, R. L., 92

"Ellen Dayton," 12
Everybody's Magazine, 45, 51

Fadiman, Clifton, 29, 85
Fairbanks, Douglas, 4

"Some Veracious Paragraphs," 89
Stagg, Hunter, 57, 58, 59
Stallings, Laurence, 58, 60
Stappenbeck, Herb, 96, 100; *A Catalogue of the Joseph Hergesheimer Collection at the University of Texas*, 100
"Steel": mentioned, 9, 10, 23, 68; the story and analysis, 80–81
Steinbeck, John, 100
"Strings and Cylinders," 98
Swords and Roses: mentioned, 5, 61, 89, 98; synopsis and analysis, 90–91

Tampico: analysis and estimate, 72–73; introduction, 71; mentioned, 5, 10, 61, 68, 85; the story, 71–72
Tarkington, Booth, 99
Tate, Allen, 91
Taylor, Jeremy, 6
Taylor, Walter Fuller, 43, 44, 95, 100
Three Black Penneys, The: analysis and estimate, 26–32; introduction, 22–23; mentioned, 2, 8, 9, 10, 11, 16, 17, 33, 35, 38, 39, 52, 62, 67, 74, 80, 98, 101
Three Soldiers (Dos Passos), 94
"Tol'able David," 32, 83
"Triall by Armes," 83
Tropical Winter ("Soirées de Palm Beach"): mentioned, 82; the stories and analysis, 84–85
"Tubal Cain," 9, 82
Turgenev, Ivan S., 6, 7, 29
Twentieth Century Authors, 89

Van Doren, Carl, 29, 42, 43, 53, 59
Van Vechten, Carl, 1, 3, 4, 10, 17, 45, 85, 94

Walpole, Hugh, 7, 43, 52, 59, 86, 87, 92, 94
Wharton, Edith, 99
What Maisie Knew (James), 52
Whitman, Walt, 95
"Wild Oranges," 18, 72, 82, 83
Wilson, Edmund, 94
Wylie, Elinor, 1, 100

Yellow Book, 6, 10
Youth (Conrad), 7